WHAT OTHERS ARE SAYING ABOUT BARRY WILMETH
AND *MAKING OTHERS RICH FIRST*

"*Making Others Rich First* will turn your investing methodology upside down. Barry's incredibly novel concepts, experiences, and strategies put you on the absolute cutting edge of enriching your life by helping others find financial success."

— David Wallace, Author of *Accessing Future Memories*

"This is the *aha* book of how we help others find their golden path to riches, and, inevitably, find ours by focusing on others first."

— Patrick Snow, International Best-Selling Author of
Creating Your Own Destiny

"If you can network, you can do this. If you have a sincere interest in the success of others, this book shows how you can provide that success. If you desire to create wealth for yourself or others, this is the place to start."

— Sonja Price, MA, ACC, Author of
Dynamo Leaders, Dynamo Teams

"You need four things to make a successful real estate deal: time, knowledge, money, and this book!"

— Matt Jenkins, Author of *Becoming a Great Leader*

"If you've ever thought about investing in real estate, or if you've made mistakes trying to climb the ladder of financial success too quickly, look at this unselfish practice. Barry Wilmeth shares experiences on how collaborating and helping others can provide the road map to your own financial wealth."

— Stephanie Zelinsky, Author of *Autistic Healing*

"Making others happy is a proven method for finding your own happiness. Barry Wilmeth shares experiences and new ideas that illustrate how this same practice can help you find financial success in real estate investing."

— Julia Matsui Higa Estrella, Author of
Being Local in Hawaii

"Barry's masterful concept is the inspiring spark that will ignite the greatness you have inside just waiting to be released."

— Lyla B. Berg, Ph.D., Author of
Leaving the Gilded Cage

"Barry combines storytelling and case studies with captivating style and a sense of involvement that you cannot resist. He illustrates an unsophisticated yet practical approach for collaborating with others to help them find their own true north."

— Lori Chaffin, Author of the
Messages Straight from the Heart book series

"This book is the Holy Grail for real estate investors who have tried and failed but want to continue pursuing the path of success in investing. These are the concepts that have stood the test of time and, until now, have never been explained so succinctly."

— Juru Dillinger, Author of *Making Love Visible*

"The true path to riches is to take the high road of helping others first. I've learned from this book how to attract all the money I need to make myself, and others, rich in real estate investing."

— Randall Broad, Author of
It's an Extraordinary Life—Don't Miss It!

"This is hands-down the best book on finding success by serving the needs of others before your own."

— Luis De La Fuente, Author of
Lessons from the Lantern

"If your 401k has fallen in recent years, or you know someone who needs to build or rebuild his or her savings for retirement, use this book to understand how real estate investors leverage private money to make 'gold mine' acquisitions."

— Bonnie Robinson, Executive Director, North Region EMS and Trauma Care Colonial, Washington State

"This genius concept of making others rich first is something every investor, novice, or veteran can do with minimum startup. Barry Wilmeth shows you how."

— Dr. Julie Miller, Author of *Secrets of Self-Starters*

"This book turns a simple idea into a fundamental strategy that changes the way you think about investing in real estate. It's a recipe for success that comes from years of experience. Listen to Barry Wilmeth prescribe all the ingredients needed to turn around your investing concepts and practices by focusing on others first."

— Tesia Melani, Author of *Upgrading Your Future*

"This book is a collection of heartfelt experiences that are inspiring, practical, and enjoyable. You'll laugh, you'll cry, and then you'll stand up and cheer! You'll be motivated to help others more than you ever did before."

— Debra Jason, Author of *Millionaire Marketing on a Shoestring Budget*

"You can be successful in half the time using just a few of the ideas explained in *Making Others Rich First*. This book is an important reference for your library—one that outlines the practices and skills for achieving goals and realizing dreams. I enjoyed it. I was inspired by it. It changed my daily routine for investing in real estate."

— Tanya Miller, Author of *Karma Over Profits*

THE REAL ESTATE INVESTORS' SURE-START GUIDE

MAKING OTHERS RICH
FIRST

CREATING
SUCCESS
FOR OTHERS
CAN BE <u>YOUR</u>
GREATEST
SUCCESS

BARRY WILMETH

AVIVA
PUBLISHING
New York

Published by:
Aviva Publishing
Lake Placid, NY
(518) 523-1320
www.AvivaPubs.com

Barry Wilmeth
www.MakingOthersRichFirst.com

ISBN: 9781943164974

Library of Congress: 2016952481

Editor: Tyler Tichelaar/Superior Book Productions
Cover and Interior Layout Design: Nicole Gabriel/Angel Dog
Productions
Author Photo: Merlie Wilmeth

Every attempt has been made to source properly all quotes.

Printed in the United States of America
First Edition
2 4 6 8 10 12

ACKNOWLEDGMENTS

I must recognize the following incredible people for being so influential while supporting my development, encouraging me to grow, and helping me to achieve greater success than I would have ever known without them.

Roger Bergeron, Terry Boren, Meredith Briscolino, Alicia Clark, Derek Clark, Aunty Hoku De Rego, Ralph Fields, Bobby Fioritto, Billy Bob Fox, John Hillyer, Phil Jones, Kalama Kim, Craig Lenhart, Rob Liles, Dale Long, John Magin, John & Lena Marthe, Sam Marquez, Dick Michels, Jim Moore, Mark Olsen, Wendy Patton, Jerry Padilla, Andy Roth, Mike Ryan, Sam Satake, John L.C. Smith, Patrick Snow, Russ Sortino, Jack Thomas, Gary Ward, Smokey Bob Wilkie, Ken Wong, and Paul Xavier.

Last on my list, but first in my heart, are my wife, Merlie Narciso Wilmeth, my mom and dad, Jim and Terry Wilmeth, and my sons, Logan and Kaipo Wilmeth. And finally, to the greatest man I never knew—Paterno Narciso.

CONTENTS

INTRODUCTION

I was in bankruptcy when I was forty-eight years old. I had never owned my own home, and I had just gotten married for the fourth time. What a catch I was, hey?

Two years later, I bought my first home at age fifty—the first home I had owned in my entire life. Over the next twelve months, I bought three more homes. Over the next few years, I bought another half-dozen. I had no education in real estate investing, and I had never attended a single seminar, so I pretty much figured I was a genius! Such naiveté!

I was on a roll until the housing bubble burst in 2007-2008. Then I witnessed a lot of people lose significantly and go underwater. They couldn't afford to sell their homes because their adjusted market value would not be enough to pay off their existing mortgages. But the bubble didn't affect me. What I realized is that I had to be doing something right and, without much forethought, that I should find a way to make real estate investing my full-time job. Again, I thought I must be a genius! But, of course, life teaches us that the more we learn, the more we realize how *little* we really know.

My first formal entry into the world of real estate investing was when I joined an investors club. Under its guidance, I went on tours, attended seminars and boot camps, gave a few talks, bought a lot more homes, and then started making a lot of mistakes. Yes, some of the rungs on the ladder of success will break! The experience kind of reminded me of taking golf lessons. It seemed like every time I took a lesson, my swing got worse and I felt more and more uncomfortable. Well, the reason for both situations was because I was practicing wrong, and I wasn't practicing correctly for a long-enough time.

It was when I started sharing my failures and successes with other new investors that my game changed. It was natural that every time I shared how to do something with newer investors, I had to do my research, use examples, and figure out how things really worked. That was the ultimate moment when I understood how little I knew about investing and how smart it is to help others get rich first. After helping dozens of others make high returns on their real estate investments, it became my forte, my modus operandi, to help others in their situations so I could learn more about how to make better deals myself. And now I want to share how helping others first is your best road to investment success.

Whether you are just getting started in real estate investing or you have been a seasoned real estate investor for many years, you can experience much more success when you help others. It's true that the more you give, the more you receive, and I can help you along that road if you are willing. Are you ready to read closely, learn a lot, expand your mind, and make this book a book to be remembered? Get ready to focus and learn how to get rich by making others rich first. But before we go further, please remember this advice above all things: Stay motivated! If you can't stay motivated on your own, team up with someone who can. Real estate investing will work—if you will!

People can be motivated by making money, or they can be motivated by making a difference! The *theme* of this book is that you should do both. The *lesson* is that you can make money best if you make a difference first. You don't have to be rich to get started, but if you have chosen to read this book, then you must believe it is time for you to start to be rich.

Statistically, only about 60 percent of Americans in large metropolitan areas own their own homes. That leaves 40 percent of hardworking Americans who have little choice but to rent. But whom do you think owns the 40 percent of the homes in America that are for rent? Believe it or not, it is mostly made up of the original 60 percent who have built equity by owning and investing in their own homes. And they may not know it, but those 60 percent who own their own homes make up the majority of real estate investors in America. God bless the USA, and God bless those who have learned how to put their money to work.

Have you seen others get in the game and win while you

felt you were still on the sidelines? Have you tried to get into the game, maybe by signing up for a FREE boot camp, only to end up paying $10,000 on the upsell? Do you think other people should go through the same experience? Or do you think others can learn from you first? All those things happened to me—the negatives, the positives, the motivational experiences that moved me from boring to soaring. If you have experienced any or all of these events, then this book is a treasure chest waiting for you to open it and use its riches to finance your future.

Most books about real estate investing will have the same basic topics, but this book is filled with the issues I have experienced that "make a difference." These topics address the most commonly asked questions I get asked as a mentor, coach, and guide. *Making Others Rich First* is designed to help experienced investors better help others realize the smartest ways to build their wealth. These are the areas that will help *you* grow by helping others first.

I didn't learn how to give because I have a lot of money. I learned how to give because I know what it feels like to have nothing at all. When you've worked hard your whole life and then a bad life experience plunges you into bankruptcy, you can either fold or get bold. I chose to define my bankruptcy as my wakeup call so I could embrace a better life. Now I want to be your coach and share with you some surefire techniques for growing rich morally and financially. Let me make it clear that you do not have to choose between the two—being moral and being financially well-off. For most of us, they are both on the same path. We become excited about getting there and even more excited about being able to "give back." How good it feels to find a treasure. How great it feels to be able to give it away.

Are you ready to begin to stretch your mind? If so, let's begin this process together. If you are excited about becoming rich, you're going to love how easy it is. If you love the idea of helping others, you will find your own success in the process. This is a book about building your wealth. People who are crazy enough to believe they can make others rich are the people who usually do. Seize the opportunity to learn with others. As Bud Fox, stockbroker, said in the movie *Wall Street*, "Life all comes down to a few moments. This is one of them."

GETTING ON THE ROAD TO RICHES

"I am grateful for the blessing of wealth,
but it hasn't changed me.

My feet are still on the ground. I'm just wearing better shoes."

— Oprah Winfrey

Few people better represent how you can go from rags to riches while helping others than Oprah Winfrey. Best-known for her multi-award-winning talk show *The Oprah Winfrey Show*— the highest-rated program of its kind in history—Oprah Winfrey has been dubbed the Queen of All Media and she was the richest African-American of the twentieth century. But Oprah didn't start out rich and successful. She was born into poverty in rural Mississippi to a teenage single mother. She was later raised in an inner-city Milwaukee neighborhood. She has often spoken about the hardships she experienced during childhood. She was raped at ages nine and thirteen, and after suffering years of abuse, she ran away from home. She became pregnant at fourteen. Her son died in infancy.

While in high school, Oprah landed a job in radio and began co-anchoring the local evening news at the age of nineteen. She got transferred to the daytime-talk-show arena because of her emotional ad-lib delivery. She became a millionaire at age thirty-two when her talk show went national. She is credited with having created a more intimate confessional form of media communication. Forbes' international rich list has listed her as the world's only African-American billionaire from 2004 to 2006 and as the first African-American woman billionaire in world history. As of 2014, she had a net worth in excess of $2.9 billion and had overtaken former eBay CEO Meg Whitman as the richest self-made woman in America.

As smart and talented as she is, Oprah did not achieve success alone. Perhaps her greatest talent is her willingness to give to others. Through the power of media, Oprah quickly learned how to make others rich first. Simply by having guests on her show, she was able to launch people's careers, make them bestselling authors, and get more and more people to tune in each day to learn from her and be impressed by her generosity. Dr. Phil, who went on to have his own successful daytime talk show, got his start as a guest on *The Oprah Winfrey Show*. Marianne Williamson, author of one of the most successful self-help books of all time, *A Return to Love*, became a household name after appearing on Oprah's show. Other books selected for Oprah's Book Club became bestsellers practically overnight. Oprah has also founded and assisted numerous charities that have endeared her to her many fans.

We can all learn from Oprah Winfrey's example. When we decide to get on the road to riches, we do so with full heart and focused intention with no forethought of not succeeding—and we embrace that the road to success does not mean leaving others behind but bringing them along with us. The first section of this book sets the stage for why we put others first and how we learn so much by helping and teaching others how to be successful.

Chapter 1

PUTTING OTHERS FIRST

*"Life's most persistent and urgent question is,
'What are you doing for others?'"*

— Martin Luther King, Jr.

We all have different ideas about what is important in life, but there are some things we all value equally. What people most want is not money. It's not salvation, and it's not freedom. It's not family. It's not safety. The two things all people want the most are to be respected and to feel appreciated. As you build your network, you will find that when you show respect and appreciation for what others do, people will flock to you, wanting to hear and benefit from what you have to share.

In others words "put others first." Find ways to comment on how you appreciate partners in your private and business relationships. When you show you appreciate someone, it's amazing how everything will change in a relationship that was once cold and you add an air of respect to a conversation. And it's incredible how even the recipient's eyes change softly when you remind him that you really appreciate everything he has done for you. As author Robert A. Heinlein stated so eloquently, "Love is that condition in which the happiness of another person is essential to your own."

Let's start this chapter by looking at the psychosocial concepts of why we enjoy helping others. I'll also share some of the life events and reasons that drive many of us to enjoy helping others so freely and purposefully.

Why We Do It—Why We Help Others

The simple act of helping others has a central place in our social life and supports fulfillment of our basic human tendencies to "do good." We cannot deny the feeling that overcomes us when we feel the need to help another person. And we cannot deny the sensation we experience when it is accomplished.

Remember the Golden Rule? *Do unto others as you would have them do unto you?* Although it is known as the Law of Moses because of its scriptural origin, this philosophy is found in nearly all religions and cultures because of its natural human calling to be social, supportive, and caring. This simple message, regardless of its origin or religious preference, addresses the power of caring for one another and the human need to do so. We like to help one another—because it's in our DNA. We feel good when helping one another—because it's in our hearts to give.

The Golden Rule is sometimes referred to as the *Ethic of Reciprocity*, which might suggest that we do good deeds with the hope of having good deeds returned to us. However, we find existentially that we have a greater need to help than to be helped. Psychologists call it "pro-social behavior"—the selfless act of helping others—even people we've never met. There is an instant, yet enduring, psychological satisfaction like few other experiences when we reach out and enrich others' lives.

We are all born with an inherent desire to grow our social connections, and research has shown that they first develop from increases in the sense of touch or contact with others. The connection becomes a healthy part of life because it helps to release the hormone *oxytocin*—which increases the bonding effect in human beings. It's a neural peptide that the brain releases when it senses a high level of comfort. We could refer to it as a "social hormone" that makes us feel trust and closeness—or a higher level of love.

Although we love to help others, and it feels good to help them, not everyone wants our help. But don't let that bother you. Not everyone has developed an affinity of trust that allows others into his or her inner circle, and many will never get there. A variety of social, cultural, and mental reasons exist for why others will not seek, ask for, or accept your help. These reasons are basically tied to social programming, a sense of self-worth, and mostly, a sense of trust.

We all trust in our early years, but through a variety of life experiences, we become more careful of whom we trust and what situations we trust ourselves to be in. For an example, let's look at the story of a little girl who trusts her daddy completely.

A little girl and her father were crossing a bridge that was a little shaky. The father was being careful and asked his daughter, "Sweetheart, please hold my hand so you don't fall into the river."

The little girl said, "No, Dad. You hold my hand."

"What's the difference?" asked the puzzled father.

"There's a big difference," replied the little girl. "If I hold your hand and something happens, I might let go. But if you hold my hand, I know that no matter what happens, you will never let go."

When we attend fraternal groups or go networking, we have a purpose. That purpose is to create relationships that develop trust. Trust is a catalyst that increases our opportunity to do good deeds and creates a bond that enables greater depth in our relationships. And when we feel trust from others, it makes us feel even more responsible because we want to secure and protect it through our actions and future involvement with them. It is only when we reach a level of trust that we are able to conduct business relations comfortably or be more intimate in our personal relationships.

Throughout your life, you will develop many relationships, but most of them will not develop to the level of trust. We don't "click" with everyone. There's a lot more that goes into creating the urge to deepen a new relationship with someone else. Those factors might include how someone dresses, his or her manners, language barriers, cultural differences, economic level or social status, or any number of others.

Enriching relationships are based on our initial impressions, ongoing interaction, and a sense of what people want versus things that people need. When we are helping others, we should strive to support their wants but be sure to feed their needs.

What do people want? People want KNOWLEDGE. People want FREEDOM. People want COMPASSION. People want FRIENDSHIP. People want LOVE. But above all, people desire two things the most: to feel APPRECIATED and to feel RESPECTED. Knowing how to manipulate the feeling of these two attributes is the single greatest way to develop relationships—to develop them to the point of moving to the level of trust.

Your newest relationships will be bettered when you provide appreciation and respect and do so in a way that the recipients "feel" it. If you give people what they need, they will never feel empty for what they want. And it is by growing relationships that we feed our own inner desires to grow.

Most of us feel *nourished* when we are helping others. In this sense, selfless acts of good deeds trigger an extremely high sense of happiness for us. Consequently, people who offer a helping hand usually tend to live longer and healthier lives, as research from psychological institutions has shown. Most of us would also agree that helping others is not only doing a good deed but being socially responsible. A good example is parenting. A family has a social responsibility to care for its young ones. The connection that develops between adults and children is appreciation where children tend to exhibit gratitude for any good deed from their older siblings, parents, grandparents, or other caretakers. In the family setting, children learn about the importance of helping others, and then they learn to practice that virtue in social settings outside the home, such as at school or at church. Therefore, social connections develop from the integrated helping skills people display.

Another important aspect of helping others is the overall *feeling of belonging* that results. For example, people would want to display the act of helping others through fulfilling allocated roles within their environment. A good example is again within the family setting; a daughter might be allocated the household chores at a tender age. In this case, the girl's parents have confidence in her ability to learn and succeed, so they try to teach her moral lessons. The girl, on the other hand, has a responsibility to obey her parents. In this case, by performing chores, the girl is able to help her parents so they can attend to other pressing family matters, such as working and paying bills. By performing the chores, the girl not only shows she is responsible, but she shows her respect for her parents and her understanding of the importance of their other duties, which benefit her as well. This, in turn, makes her *feel* positive because she is contributing to the family's overall welfare.

Of course, selfish motivations also exist for helping others; some people may want to offer a helping hand in hopes of receiving something in return. For example, members of a non-governmental organization (NGO) might want to establish a project within the community that is intended, on the surface, to benefit the underprivileged. Instead of helping the disadvantaged, however, the NGO would go one step further and acquire resources for its own good, thus taking advantage of the generous public and those most in need.

Good deeds may seem rare in our complex modern society, yet we can find instances of people doing good deeds and opportunities for us to do them all around us when we begin to look and take advantage of them. The underlying point here is that helping others has a psychological effect that creates a certain good feeling that can be taken as a reward in itself. Additionally, one good deed can lead to another by making people want to "pay it forward," thus creating a type of synergy that establishes a powerful network of people connected through inspirational acts.

Theories about evolution and the survival of the fittest suggest we are selfish; however, it is human nature to help one another. Archbishop Desmond Tutu may have said it best when he stated that we were created for "goodness." And almost all of us will agree that we have a much greater purpose in our lives than just to survive.

Regardless of our church affiliation or religious following, we all revere those who model goodness. Who can fail to revere or respect Mahatma Gandhi, Nelson Mandela, or Mother Teresa? It is basic human goodness that transcends the entire scope and variety of all world religions.

I like to call goodness "compassion." Compassion threads the golden strands of our DNA. We have an existential sense that our happiness depends on the happiness of others and that there is more happiness in giving than in receiving. We all can acknowledge as true that:

- Helping another person makes you feel better about yourself.

- Helping another establishes a connection, sometimes for a moment, other times forever.

- Helping improves the life of the giver and the receiver.

Being able to do something useful feels good! Mainly because it confirms in our soul that there is something more important beyond our daily needs and our individual self.

We humans have inner conflicting natures—one side of us is selfish and the other selfless. We struggle with that conflict daily. The selfish side has to do with survival, but the other deals with being responsible and making sense out of our existence. The first step toward being at peace with yourself is to help others first. By doing so, you will realize that you can be kind and still survive.

How do you feel when you *know* you have done something good for someone else? How warm do you feel inside when you *know* you have made a difference in even one person's life? Kindness relieves stress and fear, cultivates wellbeing, and motivates you to do more to help yourself and others succeed.

Jesus told us that those who hunger and thirst for righteousness are blessed—and will be satisfied. Indeed, we witness this sense of fulfillment when we enrich others' lives. Our lives have a greater motive than just to survive—we are motivated by accomplishing things that better the universe and make our hearts feel good.

Why I Did It—Learning from Others

I can't say I ever experienced that one single moment that suddenly changed my entire life, but I have had a number of intense experiences that made me focus on how important it is to help others. My three most eye-opening experiences were realized during 1) my military service, 2) buying my first home, and 3) collaborating with other investors on a few deals. I'll tell you the story of each of those experiences.

In the early 1970s during the Vietnam War, I was enlisted in the United States Air Force. During that time, the United States was also facing heightened racial polarization, and we even experienced actual riots on a few of our military bases.

Just months before I arrived at Travis Air Force Base (outside of Fairfield, California), the base experienced a single weekend of fighting at the enlisted club, the 1300 area barracks, and firefighter response to a transient barracks that had been set on fire. These events resulted in almost 150 arrests. Only ten people were reported as injured—but one person actually died. The lack of trust between whites and blacks, coupled with a dark atmosphere of anger, hate, and fear, fogged everyone's ability to feel safe and secure on the base for years to come.

One would think that in the military we would have a stronger sense of brotherhood integrated into our daily lives simply because we lived together in barracks and were unified by training and a mission. But remember, most of our military members had never volunteered to be there in the first place; most of them had been drafted. The Selective Service System was drafting people from all corners of the nation and placing them in a situation where they had no choice but to live with others they knew very little about while training to participate in a war none of us fully understood.

This situation created an alarming sense of insecurity for millions of teenagers who had just graduated from high school with very little understanding of the world outside the safety of their own neighborhoods. Already, we had all lost friends and family members who had died fighting in a war, the reasons for which we couldn't grasp, and now we were being trained to replace them.

In addition, the Selective Service allowed college students (mostly white) to avoid or defer being drafted. Consequently, those of us who were drafted were united by the fact that we were the ones without "opportunity." Understandably, we felt we were being treated like second-class citizens.

To make things better, we attended mandated seminars titled "Race Relations." They were half-day seminars created to "cope with the racial turbulence" then afflicting the U.S. Military. And we were actually rated in our annual performance reports based on our race relations skills. The seminars' goal was to allow us to talk freely and get things off our chests in the hopes that if we really understood what others thought, we could get along better.

One game we played in Race Relations classes was called "Stars." At the beginning of the exercise, all forty people present were randomly given a bag containing one to twenty stars. We were then placed in groups with individuals who had the same number of stars. Everyone had at least one star, but it was rarer to have two and even rarer to have three, and so on. The people with the most stars had the most power, and were, consequently, in the minority, but they could make the rules, confer taxation, and regulate the laws. It didn't take long to realize how the power of a few can corrupt a society of lower and middle class persons.

Being a two-star person, I advocated that those of us with only a few stars combine our stars together to enable our group to slip the surly bonds of social stratification and collectively overthrow the establishment. I went from person to person and gained increased support to provide social change. Our group essentially gained success as we pushed for equal laws for all—despite the select few's higher star count.

My campaign was not completely successful. Many just said, "No," or "I don't need your help," or "Just leave me alone." In a strange way, what they were saying made sense. I got it. A lifetime of living in an environment where change never seemed to happen would tend to perpetuate the rationale that it is best to seek your own security and not choose to trust those outside your circle. Many of them would only work with those who shared the same number of stars as them. That's the reason why gangs are so powerful and membership in them can be desirable—because many individuals can only find security and strength when they are unified with others of a like cause.

One of life's greatest lessons was handed to me that week. I felt how painful it was to feel anonymity and repression—without a sense of hope. I'm telling you *I felt it*. I didn't just read about it, hear about it, or listen to stories about it. It hit me in the face; it seriously changed my heart. It was my first major aha moment, and it changed me forever.

I went overnight from being an irresponsible, directionless teenager to understanding the need for self-improvement, health, a sense of spirituality, and why working together with others is the most positive path for improving myself.

All of a sudden, I was teaching Sunday catechism class-es on base for the youths, I enrolled in evening college courses, I participated in a downtown church's choir, I played softball, and I was learning how to box. I had never participated in any of those things before. Although I was still not mature enough to be in leadership positions, I was engaged in and genuinely concerned with helping others. And by helping others, I discovered I could be more resourceful and enrich my own life.

Luckily for me, the U.S. signed a peace agreement in January of 1973, ending our long involvement in Vietnam, and most of our troops returned home quickly. A month later, the first prisoners of war (POWs) began returning to the safety of our shores. Many of them made their initial landing a short distance from the 916th Air Refueling Squadron I worked in at Travis. I was present for almost every flight that came in. It felt like a duty I owed these POWs—to witness the return of so many heroes who had given all they had and endured so much.

I witnessed the now-uniformed ex-POWs walking off the plane one by one, each one's name and the length of his or her prison time announced over a loudspeaker. At such moments, even the toughest of soldiers sheds tears. We watched as these partially broken heroes hobbled down unsteady aircraft steps. Some kissed the tarmac, inspiring us all with their courage and gratitude to return home. And their excitement when they saw their wives and children run to them from out of the crowd for a hug made everything inside of you stand up and cheer. Even though our military efforts were overthrown through failed political ploys, each of these great men had returned to our shores with honor. Sharing in those moments is an experience I will carry with me all my life.

A war had come to an end. I can never forget how relieved so many of us were knowing that we could be safe to complete our military commitment without the fear of being deployed to unknown jungles in far off lands.

After the POWs returned, my father finally retired from the Air Force. He had a commanding presence, and you could feel the strength of his character, having served the majority of his military service in combat and combat support. He had spent his early career fixing aircraft engines, and then, as the Vietnam War escalated, he had cross-trained to become a loadmaster. He served countless missions in and out of Southeast Asia, and he was involved with many rescue missions during the fall of Saigon when we quickly and chaotically airlifted our military and civilians (Americans and Vietnamese) out of harm's way. For me, there is no larger-than-life hero than my dad.

I spent a full twenty years in the Air Force enduring deployments in different locations; I'm still not exactly sure why, in many cases, we were there. I was approaching my twenty years of service about the time Iraq invaded Kuwait, which resulted in the massive U.S.-led coalition that thwarted the invasion but resulted in the first Gulf War. This time was a complete flashback to when I had first entered military service during the Vietnam War. My hunch was that the situation would only get worse and we would all be deployed again. Not afraid to serve, but weary of these global involvements, I decided to retire about the time we were establishing the no-fly zone.

I was immediately hired for a civilian program in which I worked for a high tech company that manufactured digital Air

Traffic Control switches. Less than a year later, my hunch proved correct. All normal active duty positions were being converted to deployment positions as U.S. forces began the dreaded cruise missile attack on Baghdad. It took ten more years to push Saddam Hussein out of power, and almost another ten years before we officially pulled our troops out of Iraq. Ironically, that was the year I bought my first home.

Home ownership had never been a top priority for me before. Renting was my way of life, but now living a normal civilian life, free from temporary duties in foreign lands, I began to realize how important it was for me to accumulate money in my middle-aged years to take care of eventual needs once I was retired.

The first time I bought my own home, I was retired from the military, in my fifties, and had no life experience or exposure to investing, mortgages, or wealth-building concepts. That was in 2003 when mortgages were the lowest (at that time) in recorded history—about 5.85 percent. My wife, Merlie, and I bought a condo in Pearl City, Hawaii for $170,000, giving us a monthly mortgage of about $1,000 a month. Transitioning from being a renter to a homeowner was one of life's most satisfying moments. Little did I realize that I had just taken my first step toward building wealth.

I got interested in real estate investing as soon as I was actually living in my own home. That's all it took. The lure was the dream. The idea of moving from lower middle class to having my own multi-million-dollar group of assets was motivating, exciting, and something I believed I could do. Sound like a familiar story?

I was so excited with how easy it was that, over the next year, we bought three more properties and rented them out immediately. We actually had renters paying our mortgage. I thought I was the smartest guy on the planet. To this day, the advice I always give new real estate investors is that the first step to success is buying your own home.

Merlie and I continued to buy more condos and rent them out until the housing bubble burst and a global financial crisis began in 2007. At that time, I had decided to change my investment scheme and buy homes because it was the best time to buy with cash and put renters in more properties. I promised my wife I could increase our monthly cash flow by $1,000 a month within two years without taking on any new mortgages, pulling any money out of savings, or using credit cards.

I only asked that when I completed the deal, I would get a new car—a top of the line Beamer! It would be my reward and keep me motivated to complete the task. I had a vision, and I was never so focused on accomplishing a task as I was then. Admittedly, a lot of ego and pride were involved, but the objective factor was the $1,000 a month gain.

I immediately began traveling to cities on the mainland (what we call the continental forty-eight in Hawaii). I knew nothing about flipping properties, but I was sold on the idea, and the only way to get experience was to buy, rent out, and do it over and over again until I reached my $1,000 per month objective. In eleven and a half months, I had achieved my objective, and I couldn't wait to show the numbers to my wife.

Her reply was, "So now you're going to get the new car?"

"No," I said. "I changed my mind. I don't want a new car. I want to quit my job!"

She did not reply, but her raised eyebrows were begging me to explain. So I did. I told her my *goal* was to quit my job, and my three *objectives* were to:

1. Put the equivalent of one year's salary into a savings account.

2. Make more passive income monthly from rentals than I was making monthly at my job within twenty-four months.

3. Become 100 percent debt-free within twelve months.

It seemed reasonable and attainable. It took me almost sixteen months to complete all three of those objectives. I was able to leave my corporate job—a job I actually loved. That was my second aha moment. Quitting my job changed a lot of things in my life. I now had free time to do nothing but pursue building our family's wealth. And I was also headed toward my third objective: the reward of helping others to get rich. Many people wanted to work with me and help their money to grow as well. That seemed a daunting and risky situation I was reluctant to enter into. I began by showing them exactly how I completed my deals, and I explained the "Knowledge, Time, and Money" principles I will reveal in Chapter 2.

The concepts were well accepted and easy to understand, but the risk of owning property in other states as far as 5,000 miles away was too much for most. Some did their own deals directly, but many chose not to. Since these people were afraid to buy, my next step was to show them, step-by-step, how they could grow their money by 40 percent per deal. Yes, that's a big number, and every person who invested made at least that much profit. Many made multiple deals.

The basic model I use is to take investors' cash (or money from a retirement account) and purchase a home, fix it up, and sell it on my new and improved model—the Lease with Option contract(s). I use their money to buy. I make a profit on the sale and the monthly lease. At the close of the deal, the investors get their original investment back, plus 40 percent. Oh yeah, I keep everything else. Many times it is a significant gain. Sometimes, I make much less than the investors. But that's all part of the game of leverage and the ups and downs of a real estate deal.

Helping others get rich first can make you a lot of money. Yes, it's a lot of work at first, but as with anything else, over time you become very good at what you're doing. After about twenty of those types of deals, I began doing one-on-one counseling for those who want to learn how to make deals on their own. Everyone I help also helps me in one way or another. Never once have I counseled another real estate investor and not learned a little bit more about the business and about myself. The work I put upfront can be challenging, but the rewards in education, skills, and money make every deal a great deal.

Helping others this way requires leveraging resources that I don't have enough of on my own. I have never charged a fee for anyone to learn from or collaborate on a deal with me. My return on investment, however, is both subjective and objective. I'm a better person and I make money.

Learning by Helping

Helping others to grow is good for the world, and it's good for you. If you can show someone how to save money, fix a broken stove, or build a toy car, you can actually learn a little bit more about yourself.

For thousands of years, humans have found that the best way to understand a concept is to explain it to someone else. "While we teach, we learn," said the Roman philosopher Seneca.

What I quickly figured out in explaining investing to others was that by helping them, I was making more money, budgeting, and spending my time more wisely. All the while, I was learning different solutions, shortcuts, and less risky ways to get my own deals done.

Renowned nuclear physicist Frank Oppenheimer conducted research during the time of the Manhattan Project and, among other scholarly and respected researchers, followed the well-known Latin principle *Docendo discimus*—"The best way to learn is to teach." When you teach something, you have to break it down into tiny manageable pieces—simplifying it in your mind and making it easier to comprehend. The litmus test of understanding a concept is that you are able to express it in your own words. As a matter of fact, the more you teach the concept, the greater clarity you attain because the iterative process of teaching will reinforce your own understanding and cause you to develop a more effective learning system. If you want to learn anything—whether it's a new language or a computer program—find a friend you can teach it to—that way, you'll be able to learn more information, be better prepared to use it, and help another person out as well because he or she will feel good about being able to help and will come to understand the subject better as well.

Helping others is a key virtue. During difficult or catastrophic times, stories of people who have helped others are motivating, and many have far-reaching effects, such as helping the country recover from national debacles or terrorist assaults. Some men and women even commit their lives to helping other people, from the police who safeguard our urban areas to the firefighters who rescue people from blazing structures.

However, helping other people should not be constrained to traumatic situations or times of tribulation. We should help others every single day. Furthermore, helping others is also a way to help yourself. When you help somebody, that person will be more willing to help you when you need it. People are far more willing to help you when they know you would do the same for them. You may not always get to repay the person who helps you or vice-versa, but when you help enough people, you will never want for help when you need it.

Too often, karma is described in a negative context. We are told that our bad deeds will follow us, but astonishingly, our good deeds, done with the right intention, will also return the favor. Helping others to achieve something will eventually help us in understanding the know-how of that subject matter. When you're helping other people, you will frequently feel better about yourself, improving the probability that your next experience will be a constructive rather than pessimistic one. Helping other people ought to be a characteristic expansion of each business pioneer's obligations. Lamentably, helping others is not as simple as you would think. As practitioners, we regularly get too caught up in operations or our own issues to find time to assist others. Therefore, we need to set aside time to mentor or help others as one of our key goals of being in business.

Another positive of learning while helping is that learning changes the mind permanently and for the better. However, no amount of reading, researching, or educating will have any effect if the learner is not persuaded that he or she needs to make changes to his or her thought patterns. To learn and change, you have to accept that there is a gap in your knowledge or abilities that merits filling.

Nor is helping other people generally simple. It can occasionally wreck your timetable and cost you time, cash, and different assets. It can even be deciphered the wrong way. However, most people understand that time is valuable, so when you take time out of your day to help a friend, that person will remember it.

A perfect example of the power of helping others can be

found in Craig Newmark's story. In 1995, Craig was a pretty simple guy searching for ways to spruce up his life. He started an email campaign proposing that people should share information rather than search for it themselves. He began by sharing pretty simple information about high tech events and the arts in the Bay Area. That could have been the dead end of his emails, but what he started began to expand.

Those whom Craig emailed sensed the usefulness of what he was doing and quickly jumped on the bandwagon. Recipients began adding to the listings in hopes of helping others also. They added information on apartment rentals and new jobs available in the area. In just a few months, the email lists had reached over two hundred people—not so big by today's standards but pretty phenomenal in the mid-1990s. Today, that information email has transformed into one of the world's most heralded websites—Craigslist. And it continues to provide relevant information in the most popular categories where others search for help.

What Craig helped the world understand is the power of sharing in networks. And networking provides powerful forums for distributing information, getting referrals, and sharing information with like-minded individuals and entrepreneurs. So never underestimate the power of helping others—it can go global and enhance your life and the lives of all those around you.

Summary

In this chapter, we explored how we can learn more about our business if we help others grow in the same business. We experience a wow feeling that is heavenly when we feel the need to help another person. We feel good when we help others achieve their dreams and goals. Humans even release a hormone when they help others that increases the bonding effect between them. Helping also aids in developing a sense of trust between people. Hopefully, by now, you are convinced that helping others will help you. In the next chapter, we'll begin to look at specific ways you can apply the concept of helping others so it affects your daily thoughts and behaviors in a positive way by changing how you think.

Chapter 2

CHANGING THE WAY YOU THINK

"Change your thoughts and you change your world."

— Norman Vincent Peale

It takes three things to make a real estate deal: knowledge, time, and money. You need to *know* what you're doing. You need *time* to find and organize a deal. And you need *money* to consummate the transaction. Understanding these three factors will help new real estate investors have a better vision to see the deal from beginning to end. Let me explain briefly the importance of each one.

Knowledge is necessary not only to understand how a real estate deal works but to assemble the information required to work a deal. Believe me—every deal is different. Every dealmaker is different. A new challenge will arise with every deal. You can't put a deal on automatic—you'd lose every time. Deals vary so much that you will learn quite a few things on every deal you do.

Time is required if you want to make deals. They will not fall into your lap. You have to spend a lot of time cultivating relationships, working the processes, weaving together the deals and dealmakers, and communicating constantly with potential investors. Just like any sales job, if you can only do it part time, you'll never be as successful as you'd like to be.

Money is where most new investors fail. It's not because they don't have the money; it's because they don't know how to access and use money wisely. Even more, they lack the experience and polish to explain to those providing the money exactly how it will be used and returned.

In this chapter, we will discuss how understanding these three factors will change how you think about deals, deal making, and helping others. Don't be afraid to change the way you think! We usually get exactly what we expect, and by changing your expectations, you can change your world, so allow yourself the time to focus on enlightenment! You're not just a rising star—you're a shooting star. It's your time to rise and streak across the universe.

Gaining Knowledge and Skills

Knowledge is essential for any business' survival. It is even more crucial to thrive and succeed in life. Knowledge lays the framework for the skills you'll need to develop, including negotiation, analytical, and interpersonal skills.

As a real estate investor, what you earn is a function of what you've learned. Although money will come and go, the knowledge and skills you gain are yours forever to use for as many deals as you make.

When gold was discovered at Sutter's Mill in California in 1848, there was a mad scramble to dig, pan, or mine for instant wealth. However, less than 1 percent of those who traveled there actually gained any wealth. But guess who did get rich—the people selling shovels, candles, pickaxes, and tents. Local merchants leveraged their knowledge of people's *needs*.

Personal computers were introduced in the mid-1970s and provided high tech information processing to an insatiable consumer market. But it wasn't the computer developers who became the richest. Nearly all computer manufacturers failed. But guess who did get rich—the people selling computer furniture, software, modems, tutorials, printers, and storage media. Again, those who knew what people needed were the ones who flourished.

If you truly want to gain knowledge about real estate investing, you will find your niche. You must know your market, and you should know your consumer.

While you should understand and remember a lot of things about this endeavor, some specific things you must know and/or implement and *never forget* are:

- The market value of the properties you buy or sell

- The need for a formal business plan or business strategy

- The contracts you will be using

- The necessary due diligence on every deal

- To use title insurance and know the title history

- The types, terms, and sources of loans

- Your exit strategy on every property you buy

- The cash flow of each property you own

- To use a home inspector separate from your contractors

- How to leverage other people's money

- The taxation strategy you are involved with

- Never to delay evicting bad tenants

- The demographics of the market in which you are working

- Your payoff terms if you are using a loan or mortgage

- To carry property insurance and have an asset protection plan

- A backup plan

The best way to keep track of these *must-know* items is to write them into your business plan or, in abbreviated form, your written business strategy. But don't forget: Knowledge is only one of the three factors it takes to make a deal. You must also have the time and the money to do the deal.

Managing Your Time

This entire chapter is about understanding the three factors it takes to make a deal: knowledge, time, and money. You can *learn* all about how to construct a deal, but if you don't spend a lot of *time* putting together deals, you're just not going to be as successful as you should be. To be honest, the time spent may reveal the sobering fact that it is *not* a deal. In other words, attention to detail and lots of research and phone calls are time-consuming events that many disregard—so, eventually, they may fall into a deal they should have done more research on.

Also, understand that if you work at real-estate investing *part*-time, you are probably going to find the "second-best" deals. Time is of the essence! Smart deals are found quickest by smart investors who understand the importance of getting into a contract right away. I have found that getting into a contract quickly is key—while ensuring you have a contingency built into the terms so you can get out of the deal. If you're not first in, you're left out.

You may have no other choice than to begin as a part-time real estate investor, just as most people have done. Just know upfront that it's going to be a challenge to find enough time to get the best deals. You can make up for it by dedicating a few hours every day to being on the phone. Yes, the phone. Not email, not text messaging. Get on the phone and become a real estate evangelist so you have lots of people to talk to. Regardless of working full-time or part-time, you're going to have to sacrifice some other things and give it your all. And that may cost a lot—but the only thing that will cost more is *not* giving it all you've got.

The best way to spend the available time you have is studying, attending seminars, hanging out with other like-minded investors, practicing putting together deals, learning the lingo, and understanding the processes and numbers. Believe me, you will have no problem filling up your time with real estate matters. Whether life is allowing you to work full-time or part-time, you see how valuable your time is and how important it is to find ways to manage it wisely.

Developing effective and efficient strategies for managing your time is of great importance. You need to balance the contradictory demands on your time to study, vacation, make money, do business, and fulfill whatever other commitments you may have. As bestselling novelist Christopher Rice puts it: "Every day is a bank account, and time is our currency. No one is rich, no one is poor; we've got 24 hours each." Truly, how we spend our time is more important than how we spend our money. Many times it seems there is not adequate time to do everything you need to, which can lead to a lot of stress. Identifying ways to manage your time allows you to regulate your routines and design your behavior to reduce whatever form of time-related stress you are experiencing. Effective steps for managing your time include:

- **Use a To Do list on your phone or computer:** As an essential part of action planning, create a daily list of responsibilities that need to be done. Prioritize the items into *important* or not important or *urgent* and non-urgent. This, in short, means prioritizing.

- **Set your goals specifically and clearly:** Make sure your goals are realistic and achievable. You have to scrutinize the present situation and assess what goals to set and what actions you need to take to achieve them. Also, have a contingency plan for reaching your goals just in case you have to change plans.

- **Do your daily tasks and respond to queries quickly:** As they say, procrastination is the thief of time. It is imperative to manage that fear of doing things you don't want to do and understand that fear is often far worse than any possible negative results.

- **Break down your goals into smaller tasks:** By breaking your goals into smaller tasks, you can accomplish them one step at a time. In addition to remaining motivated, reward yourself when you accomplish your goals.

- **Persevere:** Inevitably, things will not always run smoothly

as you progress toward your goal, so learn how to persevere and maintain a positive attitude when things are not
going as planned.

- **Eliminate unnecessary time-wasters:** Identify some of
your daily tasks that are not contributing to your goals and
taking up too much of your time. As much as possible,
remove them from your schedule.

If you are going to be a real estate investor, you must educate yourself on a variety of transaction types, learn how to source
and sell deals, and effectively manage your properties. You'll have
to juggle a number of hats you'll wear as a marketer, negotiator,
and business owner, not to mention sometimes as a handyman and
home cleaner.

Time spent unwisely will sabotage your business' success
and quickly cut into your profits. So which activities are considered to be a drain on a real estate investor's time? More importantly, how can you manage these activities in a way more conducive
to your bottom line? Let's review a few time management considerations that might help.

One of the best perks of working for yourself is that you
are in complete control of your work schedule. The fact that you
will be working flexible hours from home and on the road is one of
the biggest reasons why you need to look closely at how and when
to do things. The more consistent your work schedule, the more
organized you can be with the rest of your time. If you are not dili-

gent about how you use your time, you could find yourself bogged down with tasks that prevent you from using your time wisely or efficiently. Most real estate investors never imagined they would be spending most of their time tethered to a desk filling out timesheets or answering phones all day. It's not that you are "above" these jobs; it's just that they may not be the best use of your time.

I can't say enough about how many times I've seen new investors go through the numbers over and over to the point that analysis paralysis has set in. I know it's exciting when you are making your first couple of deals, but be careful not to develop bad habits and overthink everything.

Time in your business is valuable so you need to know when not to overextend yourself on less important matters. It is also important to prevent or avoid mindless distractions and unnecessary demands on your time. My major weaknesses are spending too much time on my Facebook account and forecasting numbers on potential deals.

Stay mindful of the top tasks on your To Do list. Don't let yourself get interrupted with phone calls or interesting looking emails or texts that draw you away from your most urgent accomplishments. Always complete the most important tasks as early in the day as possible when you're most alert and still excited. Protecting your time is crucial for productivity, and no one else is going to do it for you.

Finding the Money

Most entrepreneurs, or folks who attend a seminar, think they are immediately armed with the knowledge and skills to do deals right away—until they face the cold reality that they must have money to make it happen. Please do not get caught up in the hype that you can buy without money. Sophisticated investors have connections to make this happen, but if you're just beginning, this is the quickest way to find yourself underwater or involved with an illegal activity.

As mentioned previously, it requires knowledge, time, and money to make a real estate deal, but the secret is—*it doesn't have to be your money*. It does not take long for new investors to realize that funding is the long pole in the tent and requires contacts, referrals, systems, and methods to source the funding needed to make a real estate deal.

I want you to know it is *not* hard to find money to complete real estate investments. But I also want you to understand that you *must* know how to put a deal together and present it smartly. Attending a wealth-building seminar does not compare to a history of making deals.

It costs money to use other people's money (OPM), and when you first get started, you will be seen as a high risk—at least until you prove yourself as someone who can put together smart deals. But on the upside, *cash* can help you make acquisitions at a lower price (money talks), make them happen quickly, and erase the need to qualify financially for a mortgage.

Many options exist for "finding the money." Here are the four primary methods that a new investor can become active with:

1. Collaboration

2. Private Money

3. Credit

4. Crowdfunding

Let's look at each one in detail.

Collaboration: Collaboration is the most common option. Most of us find our first source of money through family and friends. This is usually termed "private money," which we'll look at next.

Outside of family and friends, hard money loans from other investors are another very good source for funding. Hard money will cost you a pretty penny, but it is certainly worth it if you are flipping short-term and building your own capital.

Hard money can typically cost you up to ten points and often requires 15 percent interest monthly, plus there may be heavy pre-payment penalties. Lenders will expect around 70 percent loan to value (LTV). A seasoned investor who uses hard money over time becomes a lesser risk and can eventually have access to money with no points and less than 10 percent interest.

You could think of hard money, or even private money, as a short-term bridge loan used to get you from one step to another. The first occurrence of private money is almost always family or close friends to whom you can explain your great deal and look for a sympathetic ear. Private money is not that hard to find and not too difficult to use. However, with collaboration from hard money, there is a lot to know or establish in the numbers, the note, and the fine print. You might be able to get angel investors to support your cause, but you have to be accountable; you will be forced to explain the deal in a lot more detail and defend every decision you make since they usually won't allow you to take full control. Investors can also access funding through large web-based lenders such as:

- Realty Shares: https://www.realtyshares.com

- Connected Investors: https://cix.connectedinvestors.com

- Real Estate Angel Investors: https://angel.co/real-estate-1/investors

You can simply google "web-based lenders," "private money lenders," "hard money lenders," etc. and find a list of lenders you can contact to see whether your option, credit, and investment will meet the risk requirements they have established.

Private Money: Private money is funding secured by a note and/or deed of trust from private individuals, friends, family, IRAs, or any source other than institutional or conventional means—such as a bank. It is sometimes referred to as *hard mon-*

ey, but it is definitely different. Private money is usually relationship-based while hard money is usually from an established company that specializes in lending.

How much should you pay for private money? That is a good question. I believe it's less critical to be concerned about "how much" you pay than with "how available" it is. Nothing is worse than getting down to a close, only to discover your lender doesn't have the funds immediately available. Money usually costs 0-10 points at the time of origination, with monthly interest from 6-20 percent. The numbers I strive for are 10 points and 15 percent. Money is readily available at that cost, with loan to values around 65-75 percent. It costs money to borrow, but the question you have to ask yourself is, "What am I willing to pay to close a good deal?"

Money can possibly be secured by real estate, but more sophisticated investors will often borrow money unsecured by paying a little more in interest.

I strongly advise that you try to borrow without having pre-payment penalties in your note. Very likely, you may complete a deal earlier than you expected and you would like to pay off the loan as quickly as possible. With a pre-payment clause, you could end up losing a lot of your earnings in the deal.

One of the great things about private money is that you can pretty much find money for a host of different types of deals. You can get into deals that many traditional lenders would never touch.

And you can get into them without qualifying financially, so credit may not even matter. The lender depends on the asset or cash flow to repay the debt.

A great thing about private money loans is that they don't show up on a credit report, unless you want them to.

Search online and you will find lenders advertising private money available. I have always just gone straight to the source. I know it has saved me a considerable amount in fees. Whether you are borrowing private or hard money, many ways exist to find people with money to loan who will love clients like you who will repeatedly borrow funds.

Credit: You can access money directly by using your own *credit*. A home equity line of credit is a great place to find temporary money to invest in a deal. Sometimes, you can get enough cash just by using a credit card. So don't forget that your good credit can make a deal happen quickly without paying high interest and points to a hard money lender.

As you learn to do deals with other people's money, you may discover creative investment ideas that you think no one else has ever thought of before. Possibly so, but many ideas are not shared by some of the more brilliant dealmakers. Ask me how I know that!

Crowdfunding: Crowdfunding is a recent development for investors. It persuades others to provide contributions or donations through a web-based platform or social-networking site to fund a specific project, business venture, or social cause. Although crowdfunding is still in its infancy, it is promising for real estate investing because of Act II of the Jumpstart Our Business Startups Act of 2012. That act eliminated the restriction on general solicitation and Securities Exchange Commission prohibitions so that investors can now raise money from an unlimited number of accredited investors and up to thirty-five non-accredited investors. It's a whole new ball game now!

Brian Camelio, a Boston musician and computer programmer, popularized crowdfunding when he launched ArtistShare in 2003. It started as a website where musicians could seek donations from their fans to produce digital recordings. Its first successful project was supporting the development of Maria Schneider's jazz album *Concert in a Garden*. Almost $130,000 was raised, which provided her with the time and resources to compose her music and produce the album.

Further solidifying the effect of crowdfunding, her album was sold exclusively through the ArtistShare website, and it won a 2005 Grammy Award for best large jazz ensemble album. Soon, other crowdfunding platforms were launched, including Indiegogo and Kickstarter.

The first official crowdfunding website, Indiegogo, began in 2008 in San Francisco to assist people looking for fundraising support for their ideas or their business startups. How popular has it become? It was recently renamed generosity.com and has over 15 million people per month visiting it for ideas and support.

Kickstarter, based out of New York, began in 2009 and is now the world's largest platform. In its first five years, it hosted over 250,000 campaigns, with about a third of them finding great success, totaling $1.76 billion in funding from almost 10 million investors. Kickstarter has now opened projects in other countries such as the United Kingdom, Canada, Australia, Denmark, and Ireland. You can learn more about working with it at www.kickstarter.com.

Kickstarter may not be for you, but it is solid evidence of crowdfunding's success, so it should be a major consideration for you in finding money. As with anything else, at Kickstarter, you must have a successful vision and business plan to win subscribers' backing.

Through crowdfunding, investors can access deals and money directly and conveniently from their laptops or tablets. Money is always available as long as you've set up a great deal for your investors.

Putting It All Together to Make the Deal Happen

Not everyone is going to agree about how to put together a super real estate deal, but if you stick with some proven concepts and methods, you'll be off to a good start. They say that nine out of ten doctors say the tenth doctor doesn't know what he's talking about. You will get that same advice from sophisticated investors. That doesn't mean any of them are wrong, but it reveals what the mainstream beliefs are. The important thing is to do your first deals with low risk and high oversight.

Many popular and easy categories exist for new investors to get involved with. Below are some you should become familiar with. If you haven't already gained information on the following, be sure to ask about them in your investors' club meetings, check with your coach or mentor, or simply look for them online:

- **Loan Assumption:** Getting lender approval to take over an existing mortgage

- **Subject To:** You make the payments but keep the mortgage in the homeowner's name

- **Owner Financing:** A promissory note between buyer and homeowner

- **Rent to Own:** Use your rent to help offset the eventual purchase of the home

- **Lease Option:** Where an option amount holds first rights to buy

- **Land Contract:** You can get the deed after you pay the owner the full amount

When doing a deal, just like with buying other consumer goods, people invest for one of two reasons: Value or Price. In other words, buying for a low price means for some investors that they will have a higher margin of profit. In many cases, that is an illusion. In my experience, the cheapest properties I bought were the worst acquisitions I ever made. I suggest you always try to buy for value. Value usually holds; price—not so much.

If you must buy for price, I suggest one careful tactic: Have the property sold before you buy it. For example, if you find a property that, fixed up and sold at market price, is worth $150,000, and you can get it for $94,000 (yes, you can find these properties all day long!), then before anyone else finds out about the property, call your list of investors and let them know you have a $150,000 property you can sell to them for $119,000. If you can find someone who will buy it for close to $119,000, then you should buy the property and sell it all at once.

If you buy for value, you will want to set it up for passive income, meaning property that will bring you a profit every month because you know it will maintain its value over time and very likely grow in equity at a much higher rate.

From what you've learned so far, you must determine the type of deals you want to get involved with and focus on acquiring as much knowledge as you can about your acquisition method. Dedicate enough time to find the deal and then source the money. Remember, you need *knowledge, time, and money* to make the deal. The important takeaway here is that it doesn't have to be *your* money! If you can find a deal, you can always find other people with money who want their money to grow. Almost all of my major deals were acquired with OPM. They were mostly non-investors looking to make money without getting involved in the deal. Some actually forked over their 401K money and made it grow substantially. The average gain for all investors who allowed me to use their private money was an astounding 40 percent, and many came back for more than one deal.

Once you know what kind of deal you are looking for and you have resources for the money involved, you are ready to search for a deal. Are you planning to buy a piece of property to flip, or will you keep it as a rental? Are you going to buy with cash or get a mortgage? What is your price range? How much are you willing to put into rehabbing the property? What percentage below market value are you going to buy at? What neighborhoods are you willing to buy in? Are you willing to partner on the deal or go it alone? Have you given thought to helping a new investor find his or her first deal so you can learn from the deal yourself?

I have helped new investors get off to a roaring start, and I have helped non-investors grow their money. In each case, the wealth of knowledge gained resulted in a gain to my financial wealth. It is easy to put together deals and make money—but it is tough to make a difference. Giving back, paying forward, and providing a guiding light are all things we can do to make a difference. And if you help others along the way—to become rich first—you will find untold treasure in learning and adding to your own wealth.

Summary

In this chapter, we learned how to make a deal by changing the way you think about knowledge, time, and money. In the next chapter, we will focus on what the business of real estate investing is all about.

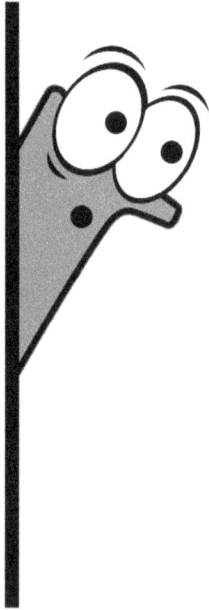

Chapter 3

MAKING THE INVISIBLE—VISIBLE

"Lucky people get *opportunities.*
Brave people create *opportunities.*

And winners are those who
convert *problems into opportunities."*
— Author Unknown

Carleton Sheets began what is arguably the turning point in infomercials for investing in real estate with no money down. He learned from real estate legend Robert G. Allen, and eventually, he ran his own "No Money Down" television infomercials successfully for over twenty-five years. Many of the methods Sheets taught were not new to investors, but they were new to the millions who couldn't get his ideas out of their heads. Today, infomercials bring in close to $9 billion in sales every year.

Sheets taught assumption of existing mortgages, seller-financing at elevated interest rates, wraparound mortgages, and even pyramid equity buying. But nothing was as attractive as his *no money down* concept.

Let's face it—for years, many prospective homeowners were short-changed because they couldn't come up with the large 20 percent down payment. They were usually able to keep their credit clean enough and were certainly capable of making the monthly mortgage rates. But that tough 20 percent down payment was the stopper.

Once reserved for only kings and nobles, owning property has long been the burning desire of the working class. What was once unknown about real estate investing to almost everyone can now be known by all. But how you learn it, and how you gauge yourself as you move toward your business goals still requires scientific methods for making the invisible—visible. Sometimes your vision needs a revision.

Getting into the Real Estate Investment Business

So first let me give you the tips and shortcuts to becoming rich quick as an investor: *There are none.* It's like the old saying, "You can't take the elevator to success. You have to take the stairs." You have to learn this business step by step. Even though you're just getting started, the smallest step in the right direction can be the biggest step of your life.

You *must* get started. You *must* get involved. And you should feel *excited* about every new step you take when getting into the real estate investing business. People usually first get excited about real estate investing because of an advertisement, a web search, a ticket received in the mail, or a book they read that they just couldn't put down. The next big step is normally attending a seminar. Seminars are, after all, very motivational; you meet a lot of different people at them and learn a lot of new terms and perspectives. Spending a few hundred bucks on a seminar can easily be a wise investment if you are going to learn several things you don't already know. Such things may include:

- Building a business plan

- Minimizing your taxes

- Wholesaling properties

- Learning how to amass passive income

- Building a dream team

- Learning how to get private money

- Meeting other investors on the same crusade

Let's look at some of the many ways of making money in real estate. Some entrepreneurs work on short-term innovative ventures, whereas others invest to secure profits for the long term. One of the best reasons to invest in real estate in America is that it allows you to take on more leverage. You cannot get a loan from a financial institution to buy stocks from a company, but getting a mortgage on a house is totally acceptable to financial institutions. Once you acquire a loan, you can just make a down payment on the house and earn rent income from it, while paying off your mortgage. Moreover, it must also be noted that houses appreciate quickly, and home appreciation is the area where additional profits can be made and realized. This is basically the American Dream—to own property and have a secure financial position even though you started off with nothing!

Since a real estate investment is classified as a huge and long-term investment, an investor must make an educated decision while starting off in this field. Here are three of the major ways you can invest in real estate:

- **Buy rental property.** This is the most basic form of investment where you take a mortgage on the property, rent it out, and charge enough rent to cover the mortgage payment and have a profit.

- **Flip properties.** Buy low, sell high—so the saying goes. The gist behind this form of investment is to purchase properties for short periods and flip them for profits. As a trader, you do not have to make improvements to the properties since you are not interested in long-term profits. This is a good strategy for those investors who do not intend to pay long-term mortgages.

- **Invest in a group.** You can also invest in a real estate investment group, which works just like a mutual fund. In this scenario, you are not directly a landlord; hence, you do not have to deal with the responsibilities of one.

By now, you must realize that real estate investing is all about building wealth. Even if you choose to go into investing through the basic method of buying rental real estate, you realize that the mortgage payments will be covered by rental income, and in the long run, your main profit will be the property's appreciation. This is just one strategy you can use to build family wealth over time through real estate.

I hope you are looking into real estate investments to earn wealth based on minimizing the risk involved while also minimizing the amount of time required to manage your investment. In choosing a property to invest in, follow these three criteria:

- **Look for a great cash-on-cash return.** Most likely when you buy property, you are taking money out of your liquid financial assets—stocks, bonds, CDs—and investing it into a very non-liquid asset—real estate. Whatever you were earning before, such as 1 or 2 percent, you should strive to earn a better rate of return on your real estate properties. Buying high cash flow-positive properties can earn you decent returns.

- **Be sure it is not a high risk deal.** New developments, non-improved land, fixer uppers, etc., all have much higher risk profiles than just simply buying a nicely established cash flow rental. To mitigate risk, consider taking simple properties in middle-income neighborhoods and do your proper due diligence.

- **Invest in properties that have low hands-on needs.** Some properties just require way too much time and management to make them smart investments. Examples include vacation rentals, cheap properties in bad neighborhoods, and college rentals. Focus on creating a portfolio of properties you can hold for as long as possible and rent to credit-worthy tenants so you can commit less time to managing them.

Ultimately, your best investments are not the ugly houses you hear so much about chasing, but the boring ones that require little work and are low-risk, cash flow-producing properties. If you're doing flips, you must use a great home inspector who can do mold analysis for you, and you must have a dependable licensed contractor who can put together good teams for your investments. Either way, plenty of good properties can be found if you search wisely, do your due diligence, and make educated decisions!

A Short History of Real Estate Investing

Generally, real estate is one of the best and most ideal ways to create wealth. However, it scares many people off because there's always the mentality that one can lose big. Evidently, losing big in the real estate market is a mathematical certainty, and many people have lived to tell the story of how big they lost in a market that otherwise has been the source of wealth for many others.

The truth is that most people who lose big do so because they fail to do their part in one way or another. With the proper education and surveillance, the real estate market is a magnificent way to make wealth. Of course, there are places where the housing market is flourishing and other places where it is not so good. That makes you wonder how it got where it is.

The real estate market is one of those industries that operates on the zero score basis. What some stand to lose, others stand to gain, and as a businessperson, you have to understand that investing is always a calculated risk. If you're looking to make a profit, you have to accept that sometimes you may end up on the losing side.

When Carleton Sheets started running his infomercials to educate people on the real estate market, the housing market then could be compared to a toddler still learning the art of balance and walking. Sheets' "No Down Payment" television program won numerous awards for its efforts to educate the general public on the real estate market. It continues to be one of the longest-running programs of its kind.

After Carleton Sheets became a full-time investor in 1970, he worked in the private sector for about ten years. He continued to be tremendously successful as a real estate investor, and he also took pleasure in teaching classes for the National Association of Realtors. He went on to create and expand his own brand of education, and then he produced his own home study material that extended his reach to the real estate investors' community. The material was based on his real-life experiences in the real estate market, and his motive was to ensure that most of the Americans who wished to invest were conversant with the various "must knows" of the housing market.

In 1978, the housing tax was introduced. Section 121 allowed for a $100,000 one-time elimination in capital advances for sellers who were more than fifty-five years old at the time of sale. Although the exclusion was increased to around $125,000 in 1986, the Tax Reform Act eliminated tax deductions from interest payments made using credit cards. The Taxpayer Relief Act that came into play in 1997 repealed Section 121 and replaced it with a $500,000 exclusion for married couples and a $250,000 exclusion on capital gains for single individuals who sold their homes. The exclusions were available every two years, which enabled and prompted most people to purchase expensive and exotic fully-mortgaged houses. Additionally, they could also invest in a second home and additional properties.

Deregulation started sometime in the 1980s when the financial world was heavily regulated by the Glass-Steagall Act, which separated investment banks from commercial banks. Deregulation allowed for too many mistakes, which inevitably led to the housing bubble crash of 2007 and easy credits considering that people could use the adjustable mortgage. Deregulation then came under harsh criticism by some economists. However, another group of economists, politicians, and analysts argued that the bill had nothing to do with the crisis that the American real estate market found itself in.

The mandatory loans were later labeled by Republican Senator Michael Rubio as "a reckless government policy." They were also believed to be one of the causes of the ripples experienced in the real estate market. The Housing and Community Development Act, implemented in 1992, established an affordable loan purchase mandate regulated by the HUD for Fannie Mae and Freddie Mac, which were, at the time, government-funded entities. These government entities struggled to satisfy the loan order and eventually announced that they were giving loans to people with low incomes and very little loan commitment, totaling $5 trillion in minority loans. The real estate market continued to flounder as other banks also struggled to meet the government's requirements of lending more money to people in neighborhoods at standard poverty levels.

Excessive risk-taking by banks and the boom in the housing sector were the result of the Federal Reserve keeping interest rates low for a very long time. In the 2001-2002 recession following the dot-com crash, the Federal Reserve unexpectedly lowered its interest rates to historic lows: from 6.5 to 1 percent. Mortgages had been sold and bundled together on Wall Street to other countries and to investors who looked to earn more than the 1 percent on offer. The housing bubble was critically engineered by the rates' long-term decline.

From 2004 to 2006, the Federal Reserve raised interest rates a record seventeen times, to 5.25 percent up from 1 percent. Many economists and investors expected the high levels to be maintained. However, in 2008, the Reserve lowered the rate again to about 4.75 percent.

Enthusiasm for home ownership remains at a record high

today in America. Home ownership is a good investment and is widely embraced as preferable to renting. Another common and arguably-true belief is that a house is the best investment you can ever make, especially when you bear in mind that today housing values are at a historic high. Volatility in the real estate market has seen the market prices fluctuate, but regardless, property prices are currently at a record high.

The Hidden Reality of Real Estate Investing

Learning how to do your first deal kind of reminds me of the proverbial onion where you are peeling one layer off at a time and, sometimes, it makes you cry. The idea is to learn how to peel smartly, using caution and making wise choices.

The two answers I hear most often when I ask new investors why they want to get into the real estate investing business are "I want financial freedom" and "I want to quit my day job." Well, you can quit your day job by investing in a lot of different things: stocks, bonds, savings, mutual funds, CDs, currencies, commodities, etc. All investments carry risk, and they all carry the possibility that you could get rich enough to quit your job. We could look at all of them one by one, but since this book is about real estate, let's focus on that type of investing.

I began investing as soon as I figured out how easy it was. No one told me or coached me when I got started, but I did have one thing going for me: My wife was behind me 100 percent. I say that because you really need your family members to commit to what you're doing since you are risking their entire futures when you get involved with this business. If you don't have a full family commitment, there will be some difficult conversations later.

Even with full support, you must go into this business with both eyes wide open, and you must be honest with yourself about risk, education, and managing your money. The greatest asset you have is your character—it's your brand and makes you someone others will want to work with—or not. Selling your character as your brand begins the moment you start talking to others about real estate investing. When doing so, always explain your experience level, keep your promises, and maintain your personal integrity— then people will want to work with you.

The secret to making hundreds of deals is to use other people's money. But *the hidden reality of real estate investing is to get others interested enough in you to get them investing in you.* You can leverage your ability to find and develop deals to such a degree that others believe in you and trust you enough to invest their money in you. To get there, once again, it's all about your personal brand— what you're known for. You have to have a great deal, you have to be able to present the deal smartly, and you have to use the property itself as collateral to ensure the deal.

First focus on the money in your SOI (*sphere of influence*). Your SOI consists of the people you know, and there is likely a lot of money there for you to use. Present to potential backers the opportunity to invest in specific properties you will be sponsoring. The transaction—of receiving their money and the payback—should be set in a contract or specific promissory note.

You can agree to terms with each investor you work with. I have always agreed to twenty-four months use of money with 40 percent return—or more. For example, if I were using $40,000 for twenty-four months to make money myself, then at the end of the term, the investor was given $56,000. That's quite a substantial return, but with the investor's money, I was able to make money of my own. I was using the oldest trick in real estate—using other people's money.

With this philosophy, you will be making other people money—first! Yes, I have done this with 401K plans as well. Depending upon the deal you have at hand, you can pay 40 percent in twelve to eighteen months—or even less. You have the opportunity to develop an investment strategy to make a lot of deals and help your SOI make a lot of money. You can get rich in the process—as long as you are making others rich first.

Leveraging other people's money to buy and sell properties is, in return, leveraging the actions necessary to make both parties a lot of money.

You don't need to be a millionaire to look like one, act like one, and manage deals like one. You don't need a million-dollar business in order to behave like a millionaire and make money like one. Remember, you are a professional, so you must work on that brand. If you want to be known as a business professional, you can start right away. With every decision you make, every relationship you build, and every property you buy, be professional. You know you are doing well when you can make money investing in real estate. You know you are a success when other people are investing in you.

One of the hidden truths of real estate investing is that your negotiating strength will pull you through the best deals. Sometimes you can *find* great deals in real estate. But more often, you must help *create* your great deals through negotiation. Think about it. Whenever you buy or sell, arrange financing, obtain bids from contractors, or write out a lease, your skills as a negotiator will influence what you get and what you give up. You can get anything you want in life, but you must do more than ask. You must negotiate. Real-world negotiators go for *almost* as much as they can get. *Forget about "what's fair."* Nine times out of ten, the people you negotiate with will try to pull more chips into their own pile and leave you with less. Likewise (unless you're sporting a halo), you'll also want the larger pile. Maybe this sounds crass, but that's the way most investors play the negotiating game.

To get what you want from negotiations, you must first know what you want. First, ask yourself: Does this potential deal fit into my wealth-building goals? Does it fit within my frame of time, money, and talents? If completed, will this deal move me closer to where I want to go? Many beginning investors jump to buy a property because in some way it seems like a good deal. But before you rush into something because it sounds good, figure out whether the deal will be good for you. Evaluate the deal in terms of your longer-term personal and financial goals.

Another great hidden truth is that, yes, you should use a real estate agent every time you buy or sell a house—and that agent should be *you*!

Another hidden truth is that, yes, you should work with professionals. Skimping on short-term costs almost always ends up costing more in the long term—and it could set you up for a lawsuit. Investors often have egos that make them think they know exactly what's wrong and how to fix it themselves. A patient goes to the doctor, and as the patient touches each part of her body with her own finger, she says, "Doc, it hurts everywhere. My leg hurts, my arm hurts, my neck hurts, and even my head hurts! Doc, what's wrong?" The doctor answers, "Your finger is broken!" The same examination applies to using a licensed electrician, plumber, etc. In other words, don't assume you know everything. Use a professional!

A hidden promise, however, is not always a truth. For example, "Anyone can do it with no money down." That's a bit of a stretch. Why? Because you still require an education to know what you're doing, what the property is like, why it's being sold, and many other factors.

Prior to talking with the sellers, learn as much about the property as you can. Here's a sampling of the information you should try to discover:

- How is the property zoned? Are more profitable uses possible?

- How large is the lot? What are its dimensions and boundaries?

- When did the property last sell? At what price?

- Is there a mortgage on the property? What's the amount of the outstanding balance? What's the interest rate?

- Which school district is the property within?

- Which employers are located nearby?

- What are the neighborhood demographics? Who's moving in? Who's moving out?

- What percentage of neighborhood residents rent versus own?

- What range of rents and property prices applies to the neighborhood?

Once you have a better understanding of the property, you should find out whether the sellers have previously accepted or declined any offers on it. If so, what were the terms and price? Sometimes, agents will disclose this information. Sometimes, you can learn it from a lender, an appraiser, the sellers' neighbors, or even the sellers themselves. If a previous deal fell through, find out why. Will this past experience influence the sellers' negotiating positions with you? Don't insult, argue, contradict, or directly challenge anything the sellers say. Always hedge your differing views with statements such as "Have you considered," "It seems to me," "In my experience," "Oh, it was my understanding that," and "What if I were to...."

When sellers like you, they will help you get what you want. If they dislike you, they will favor other buyers—even though the other buyers are proposing what objectively appears to be a less attractive offer. Never come at sellers from sharp angles. Learn that negotiating an agreement is much smarter than negotiating on the price.

Let me be a little more transparent here by explaining why the terms are more important than the price. Consider the following conversation:

"Mr. Seller, I see you are selling your house as a For Sale by Owner. I have looked around and can tell that you have the nicest home on this street. I understand why it is priced a little above market price."

"Yeah, it's a beauty inside and out. You see yourself that it's worth a lot more than the current market prices."

"Indeed it is. I've never seen anything quite like it! I'd like to make you an offer. How do you feel about that?"

"Great, but before you do, we are *not* going to entertain any lowball offers. We've had other investors call and suggest outrageously low prices. We only want what the house is worth."

"No problem, Mr. Seller. You have it listed here for $255,000. Would you accept an offer of $275,000?"

"Say what? That's a pretty high offer you're making there. Are you sure about what you're offering?"

"Sure. Sure. This wonderful property is not about the price. It's a one-of-a-kind home, and I would love to own it. If we can agree to the terms, then $275,000 it is."

"Hot diggity dog! Where do we sign, young fella?"

Sounds like Mr. Seller got a great deal, right? But what's more important to a real estate investor: price or terms? To take it a step further, the real estate investor in me would buy that home (sight unseen) for $400,000—as long as the seller agrees to the terms. You see, price is easy because it's the terms that you leverage to make a great deal. What if I told you the terms were that I would pay you $10.00 a month? That would mean paying the house off in 40,000 months! That would be 3,333 years to pay it off.

This example sounds somewhat extreme, I know, but it makes the point that you should focus on leveraging creative terms. There will be deals that ask questions, and there will be deals that give answers. Only experience gained from a variety of deals will arm you with the capacity to orchestrate winning propositions.

So the hidden reality, again, is that we negotiate the deal, not just the price. Creativity is your best friend when trying to close a deal as an investor. You must practice coming up with creative terms that make the deal work for both sides. If you do that, you can close a *lot* more deals. The more deals you negotiate to a win-win, the better deals you'll find.

Know the sellers' reasons to sell. Know the property's market and rental value. Know the neighborhood and its crime statistics. Know the property's title is clean. Know how to leverage other people's money. Know your finances and monitor them closely. Know what you're looking for. Then, when you see it, strike quickly to make an offer and negotiate the terms.

Summary

In Chapter 3, we shared some insight into what can be expected from working in the real estate investing business. Next, I want to share more about how you can get rich investing in real estate.

Chapter 4

BECOMING RICH IN REAL ESTATE

*"The will to win, the desire to succeed,
the urge to reach your full potential,*

*these are the keys that will unlock
the door to personal excellence."*

— Confucius

Confucius lived from 551-479 BC. His words have re-mained unchanged for more than 2,500 years. The maxim expressed in his quote above is as true in the twenty-first century as when he originally taught it to his seventy-seven scholars. Today, top gurus are making millions of dollars a year using the exact same message. Why? So many appear to be getting rich by selling words or products or services. The truth, however, is that they aren't selling words. They are selling dreams. They are selling fulfillment. They are selling answers to the modern world's three most continuing and compelling questions:

- How do I reach my full potential?
- How do I become successful?
- Why not me?

This chapter will remind us of why we love real estate and why we still refer to homeownership as the American Dream. It will be our initial dive into the world of real estate and the corroborating factors you really need to know so you can make smart decisions, defer to others, or stay away from a deal. You must understand the processes and you must know the numbers.

Most new real estate investors are not willing to do the hard work it takes to make investing easy. The only proof I can find that you are serious about making a lot of money in real estate is if you are willing to work hard at it. You don't get great at real estate investing in a day—you get great at it day by day. Now let's talk about why it's worth it!

Realizing the American Dream

Being rich is a beautiful thing. Getting to rich—not so much. It requires focus, deliberate planning, continuous follow up, and trial and error until you get it right—or you get lucky! Those who got lucky the first time usually learn a huge lesson when they try it a second time and fail. I wish I could say real estate investing is easy, but experience has taught me that it's only easy for those who are laser-focused on smart planning and execution of a well-thought-out deal.

In high school, no one is taught about home ownership, financing, or the tax benefits of buying and selling real estate. And even though there are college courses on the subject, they provide just enough information to be called familiarization education. You can work with the best or most expensive coach or mentor that money can buy, but until you actually go through the process, it is difficult to grasp the meaning and depth of knowledge needed to understand long-term investing, amortization, and all those items listed in closing costs.

Quite frankly, most of us are not prepared financially to buy our first home until we have a few years of work history behind us. Investing in your own home leads you to understanding more about money, taxes, and equity. It opens your thought process about ways to make your money work wisely for you and your family.

Lending institutions approve potential homeowners for a mortgage based on *risk*. If you are a potential first-time homebuyer, you need to concentrate on becoming a low-risk candidate. The lender will help you on the road and show you how to minimize risk so you can get the best deal on financing. The best thing to do is to "begin the dream."

America has become the land of promise for many people. It has become a sanctuary of dreams fulfilled for immigrants from all corners and cultures of the world. It offers limited encumbrance and endless opportunity. But the fulfillment of dreams is usually limited to those who include that pursuit with goal-laden actions—being unafraid to work hard or to sacrifice heavily in time and effort.

Fulfillment wasn't meant for those looking for a free ride, people just looking for a handout, or employees working only hard enough to get by from month to month. As the old joke goes:

"How long have you been working here?"

"Ever since they threatened to fire me!"

Dreams can be a destiny you work for or a perpetual illusion of unfulfilled desires. Their realization comes through toil and perseverance while adopting principles of hard work and adapting to changes and demands. If you're not prepared to do that, then do not attempt to jump into real estate investing full time and expect to become an instant success.

More people have become rich in real estate than any other venture, so it is no wonder that owning a home has become the by-line for achieving "the American Dream." But owning a home does not necessarily make one rich. Nor does everyone see the upside of home ownership as a route to building wealth. But they should!

Having a declining mortgage, increasing equity, and significant tax deductions fosters one of the greatest opportunities to commence stepping down the path to wealth. It is the best time to "up your dream!" It's the best time to seek more out of what you are building.

As I alluded to in the introduction, most areas across America consist of a 60 percent homeowner population with a renter pool of 40 percent. So who owns 40 percent of America's housing that is being used for rentals? Most of it is owned by the original 60 percent—the people who have gotten started experiencing the American Dream by enhancing their wealth through rental properties.

Being Prepared Is Preparing to Succeed

As author Henry L. Hartman once said, "Success always comes when preparation meets opportunity." It is preparation that puts us in a position to succeed. How do we prepare to be rich? First, we need to know where we want to be before we can build a plan on how to get there. We need to know our niche and what fits our knowledge base. Let's start by defining how we want to invest, where we want to invest, and then what to invest in.

Most people get involved with investment properties for one of two reasons: 1) they are looking for passive income using a buy-and-hold strategy, or 2) they want to flip properties. Both strategies provide tremendous opportunity, so even though having diversity in your portfolio is recommended, most investors stick with the one they think fits them best.

Here is a shortlist of things that anyone who wants to invest in real estate can do to be better prepared, gain knowledge and skills, and build a network of supporters:

- **Attend real estate investor club meetings.** You will definitely find others at investor clubs who are trying to accomplish the same dreams you are and who will want to help and, in turn, help themselves. Visit http://www.rei-club.com/real-estate-clubs.php to find a club near you.

- **Find blogs you enjoy and write blogs that show you know your stuff.** Go to https://www.google.com/alerts and turn on the power of Google Alerts. Get immediate notification when any new posting occurs that is similar to the topics you list.

- **Leverage social media for exposure on your properties and services.** You should also maximize on this opportunity to build your brand.

- **Go to seminars as often as you can.** Most seminars are *free* or have minimal fees to attend. There's always something you can learn at them.

- **Learn how to network by attending various networking events.** You may attend through a number of such events before you find the one that works for you.

- **Find a mentor who will work for you and not charge you large fees.** Most successful investors enjoy giving back and mentoring new investors.

- **Partner with a successful investor.** Partnering is a great way to learn. If you are both vested in the success of the effort, you can learn as you go through the transaction.

- **Go on a real estate buying tour to see firsthand how deals are made.**

Being prepared to succeed means that you must establish your niche and acquisition preferences. People must know you for the types of deals you have expertise in. You should establish your brand as the person to call for a specific type of deal. In the next section, I will concentrate on property flipping and passive income because they are the two most-used methods for building massive wealth.

Knowing the Numbers

"Getting rich quick" sort of reminds me of Bigfoot—everyone knows what Bigfoot is, yet everyone strongly suspects Bigfoot is just a myth. Likewise, finding a way to "get rich quick" is harder than capturing a mythical beast. You can only get rich as quickly as you are able to analyze deals.

When analyzing deals, there are two very important considerations: 1) crunching the numbers to determine whether you have a good investment, and 2) determining the specific acquisitions that fit your business. There is a big difference between buying and selling single family homes versus buying and selling mobile homes, condos, or commercial properties. Likewise, different accounting methods can be used to evaluate your deals to ensure they meet your investment portfolio's goals.

Investors usually go into real estate for one of two reasons: 1) they either want to flip to make quick money, or 2) they want to have monthly cash flow—passive income. I want to address both of these and then conclude with the model I use to do both!

Flipping properties is a very popular tactic for making very good money. Basically, you are buying a property at a discount and then reselling it to another party "as is" or after it has been upgraded. You can buy duplexes, fourplexes, or even apartment buildings, but the single family home is the most popular.

If you're determined to build passive income, please understand that there is very little that is "passive" about it when you first get started. The long-term idea is to have profits coming in on a regular basis without the need to be actively involved. Untold thousands of people have tried to create fruitful passive-income streams only to be surprised by the amount of work, cash, or time involved.

Whether you are flipping properties or trying to build passive income, you need to know your numbers. As one of my mentors once said, "There are two kinds of investors in this world: those who understand the numbers and those who don't." Successful investors always know their numbers. So if you look at investments the same way successful investors do, you will know your numbers and you will know how to differentiate between good deals and those you should leave alone.

To understand what is required to know your numbers, let's look at a few important equations you should know. But before we do, you need to ask yourself the top-level question: *How do I know whether this property is a good investment?* The simplest answer is to find out what your return on investment is. And that's really what all the standard formulas are used for. They help determine mathematically whether the return you will get on this deal will fit what you are seeking. Keep in mind that many other factors will bear on a decision; we're just looking at the math element of the decision right now.

Investors use a variety of models to analyze deals, and each investor has his or her favorite. Personally, I care less about cap rates and cash flow, but I do favor yield and cash-on-cash return. So let me explain a few of these models and why some investors deem them to be important details for new acquisitions. I'll keep it simple and straightforward for now. So let's begin by discussing Net Operating Income (NOI), Capitalization Rates (Cap Rates), and Cash Flow.

Net Operating Income is important because you need to know it before you can determine the other major investment formulas. It is the final sum of money left over when you deduct the operating costs of a property from the Gross Income it produces.

For example, if you are considering the purchase of a fourplex that brings in $500 a month, then your Gross Income is $2,000/month.

If the building operating costs (taxes, insurance, etc.) would be $750 per month, then it's easy to determine the NOI by subtracting that from the Gross Income of $2,000.

$$\$,2000\ (Gross\ Income) - \$750\ (Operating\ Costs) = \$1,250$$
$$monthly\ income\ (NOI)$$

Okay, so we know, in this very simple example, that the property can net $1,250 per month of operating income. Now, how do we quickly find out what kind of cash flow we're looking at? What's the bottom line?

Cash flow is simply the money left over if we subtract the Debt Service from the net we just determined. So what is Debt Service? It's the money you pay for the debt or, in this case, the mortgage you use to purchase the property.

So if you bought the property with cash, there is no debt or debt service. If you have a mortgage, the debt service would be the principal and interest paid. For example, if you bought the property for $200,000 and put 20 percent down and got a mortgage for 4.5 percent, you'd be paying about $810 per month for the mortgage.

So NOI of $1,250 minus debt service of $810 equals $440 cash flow, right?

One further example I will throw at you is Cap Rates (no one but no one says capitalization rates). I don't use cap rates, but because they highlight a differing perspective on investing that you might find useful, I'll cover them here. Although cap rates are mostly used for commercial real estate, many investors like to see a good cap rate on residential acquisitions. The reason it is so captivating is that it actually tells a nice story on your investment and reflects *how much return you are getting on your investment.* Basically, if you divide the net operating income by the cost (or value) of the property, you would have a method for determining a rate of return that pretty much will tell you whether the purchase is worth it or not.

Using the formula Cap Rate minus NOI/Price, we can use our annual NOI of $15,000 ($1,250 per month x twelve months) and divide it by the price we paid for the property—$200,000. In this example, the cap rate is 7.5 percent, which is fine since anything between 5 and 10 percent is considered acceptable to very good. I would base a cap rate on the location and return I would get on a property. I tend to shoot for 9 percent, but I would take 7.5 percent if the property were in a good neighborhood and had a low vacancy rate.

Let's try an example to determine cash flow on a property we are interested in. As you recall, we need to determine income, expenses, and debt service. In this case, you are interested in buying a fourplex for $360,000, but you want to know whether it seems like a good deal for your portfolio.

You've determined to get a mortgage at 5 percent using 20 percent down. So that is $72,000 down payment with a mortgage of $288,000 over a thirty-year period.

Your due diligence reveals that the expected rental income would be $1,100 a month for each of the four units. Calculating $4,400 a month times twelve months gives us Gross Rental Income of $52,800 for the year. There are currently no other sources of income for this property. I always add a vacancy ratio to my properties to be realistic, so you determine that about 5 percent of the gross income will be lost due to a few times that one renter moves out and there is a time lag before the next renter moves in. A 5 percent loss makes our Gross Operating Income $45,600.

Gross Rental Income	$52,800
Vacancy rate of 5 percent	– $ 2,640
Gross Operating Income	**$50,160**

The following is what you've discovered for computing operating costs:

Property tax	$2,900
Homeowners Insurance	$1,700
Maintenance	$2,200
Public Water and Sewer	$ 800
Common Area Utilities	$ 600
Yard Service	$ 900
Advertising	$ 350
Property Management	$4, 224
Total Operating Expenses	**$13,674**

Subtract expenses from Gross Income to get Net Operating Income (NOI)

Net Operating Income   **$ 36,486**

The following is what you've figured will be paid for the mortgage:

Debt Service   **$21,455**

Subtracting expenses and debt service from income leaves us our cash flow result.

Cash Flow   **$15,031**

So what's your cap rate? It's your NOI divided by the Purchase Price

$36,486 (NOI)/$360,000 = cap rate of **10.14 percent** (Good deal!)

Knowing the numbers is very important, but the results are only as good as the due diligence you used to make sure you knew the actual numbers in each category. Sometimes, there are other expenses, and you need to know them all.

Losing It All and Finding Yourself

Those of us who have gone through a bankruptcy, foreclosure, or significant loss in an investment are actually better prepared than most. We've felt the pain of poor planning, inefficient execution, or failure to manage smartly. Failure is a real education substantiated by Rhoda Olsen's analogy, "If I didn't make so many mistakes, I wouldn't be so smart." Once we get over the emotional state of a bad experience, we eventually stop belaboring what happened and remind ourselves of what we've actually learned. And true learning doesn't take that many mistakes.

My personal bankruptcy startled me more than anything else that has ever happened to me. Throughout my life, I had always paid my bills on time and never run up my credit cards. But it only took about a year to develop an attitude of passiveness and neglect in order to ruin my financial status completely. I felt empty and like a complete loser. When I hit rock bottom, I didn't bounce very well. I fell flat on my A$$.

I was in my mid-forties with ruined credit, and I was a lifetime renter who had never owned his own home. But bankruptcy not only *startled* me—it got me *started* on a new road! You never know how hard you can work until hard work is the only choice you have. Not so much an aha moment as my wakeup call—my get out of bed call—my "get to work" call. I had to work two jobs: a regular forty-hour a week job as a training manager, and then at 5:00 p.m. to midnight, I worked as a bus boy and waiter. I was so focused on recovering that I never felt tired. As the old saying goes, "You don't drown by falling in water; you drown by staying there." I was determined to swim back to the surface. I actually started to look, for the first time in my life, at how to put my money to work. And my eyes were wide open!

You can recover from a bad real estate investment the same way you can from a divorce, the loss of a loved one, or another tragic life event. And usually, we learn much more because of it. It's a sort of healthy healing from an unfavorable feeling—a healing that makes us stronger.

The continued economic recession combined with declines in rental rates, declines in occupancy levels, other deteriorating property fundamentals, and increases in capitalization rates have caused declining property values. In the context of record levels of outstanding commercial mortgage debt, these factors place considerable stress on the ability of borrowers to service debt and to refinance scheduled maturities. While some loans might be refinanced or extended, many maturing loans will eventually result in other resolution strategies, including workouts/restructurings, bankruptcies, discounted payoffs, or foreclosures.

The real estate recovery gained momentum in 2014-2016. This was good news for an industry that had experienced a much slower recovery than after previous recessions. In fact, the recovery's pace can make it difficult to spot the signs of improvement until they are in full swing. At first glance, many of the trends identified in 2015 were similar to those identified in previous years. These trends were relevant when originally identified, but the slower pace of this economic recovery prevented them from coming to fruition in the expected time frame. The difference for 2016 is that the market has progressed further through the economic and real estate cycles; we are now seeing real evidence that the trends finally have the momentum to make an impact on the real estate market.

Going through tough financial times has the effect of tempering those of us who have lost a lot but are focused enough to recover. Many famous people have lost a small fortune only to gain a large one by responding to tough times. There's such a hard dose of reality when you lose, but you can find a way to climb to the mountaintop again. And when you do, it says so much about your true character. The only reason I bring this up is because the real estate investment business is fraught with challenging deals that look easy on the surface but may have dangers below. Great due diligence can never find everything. I want you to know that even when a deal goes bad, you can recover and make up for it. Bad deals are a part of this business, but they won't break you.

Summary

This chapter was about making sure that understanding the numbers is significant to finding the best deals and about how you must be prepared before making an offer. In the next section, we'll look at how to build your business framework. Beginning with Chapter 5, we discover how to reach a higher level of understanding—the initial building block for creating a business strategy or a business plan.

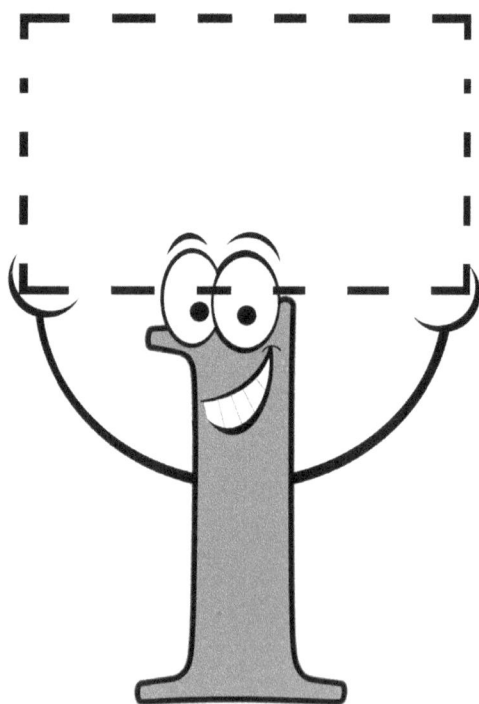

SECTION II

SETTING THE BUSINESS FRAMEWORK

"When a group of individual brains are coordinated and function in harmony, the increased energy created through that alliance, becomes available to every individual brain in the group."

— Napoleon Hill, *Think and Grow Rich*

A business framework encompasses the policies and pro-cedures, standards, and training that establish a company's culture. It includes the management structure for decision-making and the guidelines for managing risk, allotting monies for investments, training, and marketing. You must have a strategy to plan from and a knowledge base about a specific investment type so you can make hard decisions and become adept at your focal points of profit.

You may think that the business framework is not that complicated for a real estate investment business, but establishing your framework means you must decide how you will invest and what you will invest in. Are you going to flip properties or build a portfolio of rental properties? Will you be setting up a Limited Liability Company (LLC)? Who are you going to use on your team of specialists, or will you decide on that with each new deal?

If you fail to set up a framework for deciding how to grow your money, you are seriously in danger of losing your money. Just like lending, investing is all about the difference between risk and reward. Although every deal has some degree of risk, each deal can also range from small to huge profits. You've heard it before: If you fail to plan, you're planning to fail.

In this section, we are going to examine the aspects of setting up your business by making sure it is a business and not a hobby, setting goals and objectives, and establishing your business plan or strategy.

Entrepreneur and investor Scott Belsky said, "It's not about ideas; it's about making ideas happen." That is what a business strategy is. You have a goal for financial independence, but you need to construct how you will make that happen. In the heart of every entrepreneur is the desire to make it happen. I believe that if you can't write it down, you really don't understand what you're doing. So let's set the framework and begin to build on that foundation.

Chapter 5

ESTABLISHING THE GROUNDWORK

"Your present circumstances don't determine where you can go;
they merely determine where you start."

— Nido Qubien

Running a business is easy. Running a successful business is not for the faint of heart. It requires constant and consistent management involvement. Even if you start with a great business strategy, I remind you that planning is easy—execution is tough. According to the old saying, "You only have to work half days—and it doesn't matter if you work the first twelve hours of the day or the second twelve hours of the day." A major part of execution is managing things that don't go as planned. It's part of the overhead.

As a real estate investor, you may judge your business by how successful it is, or by how much money you make, but the government will judge by how legal it is being run. You don't need to be afraid of setting up a business, but you should be afraid if you're doing anything illegal. In case after case, I have found that many investors did not know they were doing anything illegal. They are truly sorry either for not reporting their taxes correctly or not providing required disclosures or complying with state laws on transfer of ownership. However, Lady Justice wears a blindfold to who you are and whether or not you know the law. She remains objective in every sense.

Creating a Hobby versus Running a Business

What is a business? How is it different from a hobby? How do I know whether I have a business or a hobby?

A hobby, as defined by the dictionary, is an activity you enjoy. If that is true, then running a business can also be a hobby. The writing of this book alone shows the difference between a business and a hobby. My hobby is writing this book because I'm enjoying it, but it also is part of my business since it will lead to my making money from book sales as well as future real estate deals from those who take my advice or invest with me. Helping others get rich first is still my hobby even if I take it very seriously. It is one thing I do at my leisure and for my pleasure. In other words, anything you enjoy doing is a hobby. It becomes a business when you make money from it on a regular basis.

Developing your hobby into a business requires you to establish your status early. Determine it as quickly as possible because it will affect your taxes as well as deductions. Failure to declare your business activities on time and determine your income could lead to fines and penalties on top of the tax you may otherwise pay to the government.

Here are some key questions to consider to know whether you are running a business or engaging in a hobby:

- Is the activity being undertaken for commercial reasons?

- Is your main intention, purpose, or prospect to make a profit?

- Do you regularly and repeatedly undertake your activity?

- Is your activity planned, organized, and carried out in a business-like manner?

If you answered yes to all or most of these questions, it is very likely you are running a business. Visit the IRS website or work with your local Small Business Administration to understand further the differences between a hobby and a business— there will be enough information and examples there to guide you.

Once you have established your hobby as a business, you will have to pay tax on the money you earn and claim deductions on your expenses. You will also need a Federal Employer Identification Number. The FEIN is required for tax accounting and administration only and is not used for purchases or sales. Your business plan should list it and your business banking account may require it. You do not need any of these if your activities are just a hobby. As soon as your hobby becomes a business, you will also need additional licenses and permits, depending on your type of business. For example, if you are running a home-based business, you may need the city council's approval.

The most important consideration here is how dedicated you are to your endeavor. If you are running a business, you will spend every available hour making sure you are making the right deal and that you understand the risk involved. If it's just a hobby, you will spend minimal time acutely studying the numbers. Then you will stand up and cheer if the deal is good or blame others if the deal goes sour.

The IRS Knows!

If you are unsure whether you are a business or a hobby, that doesn't mean the IRS isn't sure. One thing is certain. If you consistently lose money year after year, the IRS may classify you as a hobby. Its rationale is that once you are a hobby, you will be required to prove your profit motive in order to claim all your deductions. It will only allow deductions for business—not for fun things to do.

If you get audited, you'll have to prove that you put enough time into the business, where and when you made profits, whether you depend on the business' income, and believe it or not, whether you have the knowledge required to run the business. The categorical rule is that if you claim losses for three years in a row—it's a hobby.

But why should a real estate investor be concerned about that? The rationale is startling: The IRS will eliminate your ability to take the deductions you thought you had. This is the ultimate red flag for an audit, and the IRS will want to examine your bona fide business plan.

The IRS has clear rules that establish what you pay in taxes from all business or private ventures. Taxpayers are reminded to follow strictly the required and necessary guidelines when determining whether the activity they engage in is a business or a hobby (not profit-based and oriented). This explains the rules that determine whether one activity or the other is worthy of being called and regarded as a business and the limitations that apply if it is just a hobby. According to IRS estimates, wrongly-deducted hobby expenses, exemptions, and credits account for $30 billion in annual unpaid taxes.

Generally speaking, in conducting a trade or business, taxpayers may deduct ordinary but necessary expenses. An ordinary expense is one that is common and accepted in the taxpayer's trade or business while a necessary expense is one that is appropriate for the business. Also, an activity qualifies as a business if it is carried on with reasonable expectation of making profits.

Taxpayers are, therefore, encouraged to consider the following factors when making this determination:

- Has your time and effort into the activity been proven as an indicator of intending to make a profit?

- Are you dependent on income from the activity?

- Are your losses due to circumstances beyond your control, or did they occur in the start-up phase?

- What have you done to change your operations activities to improve procedures and reasonably expect to see profits?

- Can you show that the appreciation of your long-term assets will eventually turn a profit?

- Do you have the requisite knowledge to carry out your actions to establish a successful business?

The IRS wants to see that a profit was made during at least three of the last five tax years. For activities that are hobbies, deductions must be claimed on Schedule A (Form 1040).

Even if you survive an audit, you really don't want to go through the pains of proving all receipts and actions required of a business. There is no way you can win without extreme pain in the process. The best way to make sure you are running your business appropriately is to set up an LLC or other business type, consult with the Small Business Administration in your area, and have a full-time Certified Public Accountant manage your books. Overhead is the cost of doing business, so don't ignore it just to save a few pennies. Quite frankly, if you can't afford these services, then you probably are not making enough money to stay in the business of real estate investing.

Setting Goals and Objectives

To envision your success, you have to set some specific goals. In addition, setting objectives is the best and correct way to measure your path to success. Unless you have practical solutions to back up that powerful vision of yours, you cannot achieve your goals. Merely believing that you will succeed is not enough; neither is it the same thing as understanding how to get there.

Goals do not necessarily define who we are; rather, we set goals as if we were setting sail. We are giving ourselves directions toward a new horizon—to reach a state of accomplishment. And to prove we are heading in the right direction, we develop objectives. Goals are pretty much a *subjective* factor while objectives are those *measurable*, quantitative elements that provide flags of completion along the way. A musician isn't judged by how long she plays but by how well she plays. We can evaluate the musician *objectively* by measuring how many seconds she played. We can judge her *subjectively* by how well we feel she played.

Numerous motivational teachings and presentations can encourage you to dream and work to make the dreams come true. However, goals are understood as a state; for example, "being healthy." That state does not include the measurable links in the chain that ensure goals are being reached. Goals are subjective while objectives are quantifiable (they reflect positive steps accomplished on the road to the goal).

For example, a goal might be "Solving World Hunger." This is a mere state of accomplishment which, when fulfilled, would mean that world hunger is solved. To know we are on the right path and doing the right thing to achieve this state of solving world hunger, what would we need to do? Simply put, we know that by constructing quantifiable actions (objectives) to follow, we can progress in our journey toward accomplishing our goal. Here's another example:

GOAL = Quit My Job

OBJECTIVE 1: Have one year's salary—$144,000—in an LLC business account no later than December 15.

OBJECTIVE 2: Be debt-free by December 15 and owe nothing for monthly payments other than my mortgage.

OBJECTIVE 3: Have enough income each month to replace my salary—$12,000 by December 15.

We can *measure* each objective to see whether we are reaching our goals. The only way to determine whether you are heading down the road correctly to meet your goal is to have objective, measurable items to prove it. Build smart objectives and use them to help you reach your goals.

It's a well-accepted fact that in order to achieve a truly successful life, you must set meaningful goals to drive you forward to the place you want to be. But what is often not understood is that one of the essential aspects of goal setting is to attach the achievement of your goals to emotions. It is not enough simply to say, "I want to live in a large five-bedroom house with a heated swimming pool," or "I want to drive a shiny, red Ferrari." Those may be the material things you desire, but to ensure your goal is effective, you must state exactly how acquiring those things will make you feel. In fact, when planning and stating your goals, the best place to start is with the emotion you want to feel. It's no good having big houses, fast cars, and all the money you need if they don't bring you the inner fulfillment essential to your life.

Outlining Your Business Plan

You should plan the development of your business plan in two parts. First, think through what needs to be in the plan, and secondly, actually develop the plan. You may discover, once you have a solid outline, that you really only need a business *strategy* instead of a full-blown business plan.

Writing a business plan is a major stumbling block for many new entrepreneurs. They read all the articles, books, and blogs about the importance of having one, how to format it, what its contents should be—all the "do this, don't do that" stuff, and then they stress out about writing it.

If you are worried about writing a formal document, consider what U.S. President Dwight D. Eisenhower said, "*I have always found that plans are useless, but planning is indispens-able."* You are going to find that, many times, an outline is all you need to develop a business strategy. A full-blown business plan really becomes necessary when you are presenting your company to financiers in an effort to get them to invest directly with you or when you are looking for a long-term business loan or line of credit.

The point I want to make here is that for the great majority of the six million new businesses that start up each year, a planning document is not all that necessary, and it might even be considered a waste of resources. At the same time, however, *planning* is absolutely necessary for every single one of those businesses. You will want to do some pretty detailed planning, and the purpose of your planning is to develop a fairly detailed strategy that you can continually modify as you move ahead.

When planning, keep in mind that planning is easy, but execution is tough. A plan is just a plan, and it should be treated as a living document—able to move with the winds of change that will affect your business.

Here is what you need to include in your strategy planning:

- **A Strategic Outline:** You need to understand what your strategy is going to be to build your business. This outline only needs to be complete enough to manage your business—no one else (other than your advisors) is likely ever to see it.

- **The Basics You Need to Work Out:** You will need to understand your market and do whatever market research is necessary to accomplish that. You will also need to develop forecasted revenues and detailed expense estimates...both to start your business and to operate it. And, of course, the most important of all basics—you must determine how you will be using money. First, you need to determine how much you will need to start your business, and secondly, you need to define how money will flow in and out of your business.

- **Your Resources:** You should have an advisory board, or group, assembled to assist you through this planning process. Or it can be a mentor or real estate investment business coach. Whichever you choose, it can mean the difference between your business' success or failure—so use a mentor or coach, especially when planning your startup.

- **Flexibility for Constant Updating:** The less formal you make your planning, the easier it will be to make frequent changes to it, based on your ongoing experience with the business. Updating your planning frequently also provides the opportunity for you to review your thinking and see how it has changed since you first started.

So, in essence, don't sweat the thought of writing a mighty tome about your business idea unless you are looking for venture capital, but be sure to do a thorough job of planning your business.

Remember, you are always planning, but how you record your business planning is strictly up to you. Cocktail napkins, whiteboards, digital records, email trails, etc.—they all work as long as the way you keep records works for you.

A business plan or business strategy establishes the framework from which you will develop your action plan. In this chapter, we are merely *outlining* the business strategy. In the next chapter, we are going to do more work with putting it together. There are many examples of business plans available to you, and I have found that no matter where you start, the goal is to end up with something unique—something that fits you and your needs. Start with this outline and briefly fill in a short answer for each tag below. It's just a starting point. But use it in its entirety to help you focus a little better before you actually begin to write the business plan/strategy.

- Mission Statement:

  _____
  _____
  _____
  _____

- Goals:

  _____
  _____
  _____
  _____

- Financial Status:

  _____

  _____

  _____

  _____

- Target Market Analysis:

  _____

  _____

  _____

  _____

- Acquisitions:

  _____

  _____

  _____

  _____

- Team Members:

  _____

  _____

  _____

  _____

- Exit Strategies:

  _____

_____
_____
_____

- Back-Up Plans:

    _____
    _____
    _____
    _____

- Sample Deals:

    _____
    _____
    _____
    _____

When filling in your business plan, remember that a plan is just a plan. You are not going to do everything according to the plan. It is an outline and philosophic approach to what you wish to accomplish and how you intend to conduct the business.

You must also consider the types of purchases and sales (acquisitions) you will use, such as:

- Land Contracts: where the Seller provides financing at a specific price

- Lease with Option: binds the Seller to a price while Buyer is paying rent

- Seller-Financing: Seller becomes the Lender with specified terms

- Wrap-Around Mortgage: Seller finances the deal wrapping price around his or her existing mortgage

- Subject To: Buyer takes over deed and pays mortgage, but the mortgage remains in seller's name

- HUD online: Buy distressed properties on the Internet

- Tax Liens: Buy tax lien certificates to claim properties awaiting homeowner repayment or default

Define these specific purchases and sales in the Acquisitions section of your business plan and make a sample deal of each of them in the final section—Sample Deals. Many investors only want to deal with specific types of deals. So when you are looking for private money, it is important to anyone who reads your business plan to have a clear idea of the kinds of deals you are working.

Summary

This chapter helped lay the groundwork by establishing that for you, real estate investing is a business and not just a hobby. Now you should have an outline to fill in your business strategy so you can more clearly see the big picture coming into view. Next, we will look at the real business of working for yourself and further developing the business plan.

Chapter 6

WORKING FOR YOURSELF

"It's your road and yours alone. Others may walk it with you, but no one can walk it for you."

— Rumi

Working for yourself couldn't be better, could it? After all, you're finally working for someone who's not an idiot, right? You're finally able to give direction and make smart decisions, right? OK, we'll assume that the answer to those three questions is "Yes."

Working for yourself is not a part-time job, to be sure. But it's not a full-time job either. It so much more than a job—it's your lifestyle. It's what you live for! I think Mark Twain put it best when he stated, "The two most important days in your life are the day you were born and the day you find out why." When you get your own business up and running, you feel alive, excited, energetic, liberated about your "why," and as if nothing can stop you.

This chapter's opening quote is both a bit scary but also exciting because you get to do what you choose rather than be employed and told what to do and how to do it, but at the same time, you are now fully accountable and must find the answer to every challenge you face. If you want to begin real estate investing as a hobby, please do not confuse it with a business. Never! If this is a business, you must establish it as so legally. If you're going to run the business for profit, then you need to know your market and develop a strategy on procedures and accountability.

In this chapter, we'll discuss building a business plan that fits your target market and the importance of developing and maintaining a brand. I will also share some tips on overcoming any fears you may have about jumping into a new business fraught with moving parts, legal restrictions, and dependence on other professionals to help you.

Knowing Your Market

Real estate *marketing* is different from *knowing your market*. Your marketing will be done through networking, social media, meetings, and field visits to develop your brand and broaden your prospects and appeal. Market analysis is done to prepare the marketing plan that should be part of your business plan. In that section, you should be able to explain where your target area is economically and where it is expected to be while you are involved with it. You should be able to prove your market research and how investing in your target market will benefit your business.

Most businesses provide either products or services. As a real estate investor, you're not only selling both products and services, but you are also purchasing both. While your *market research* will be almost the same, whether you are investing for passive income, flipping, seller financing, or developing, your *business strategy* in that market will vary greatly and is the real decision-making tool you will be using because it sets your limitations and objectives.

One of my first business strategies was targeted at a major metropolitan area market for middle to low-income markets where I mostly acquired homes in the $5,000 to $25,000 range. The rationale was based on my limited knowledge of building passive income coupled with my false confidence that I could make this happen without any help or guidance. My market study seemed to be on target (as most investors will proudly announce), and I was able to buy all those properties with cash. The market analysis revealed that it was a market with plenty of renters and low enough inventory to ensure the properties would be fully rented out because of the low vacancy rates. But there were a number of missing variables.

The most important is that just because you move a renter in, there is no guarantee that he will pay his rent. Your due diligence should be not only on the acquisition but on how it will make money for you and on the clients and sellers who will be involved. I had invested, unfortunately, in a tenant-friendly county that made evictions very challenging and collecting damages almost impossible. It's safe to say that over 50 percent of the properties I bought in those areas lost money. Thank goodness it wasn't a loss on much more expensive properties. On one hand, I received a very strong education on buyer-seller relationships and the legalities involved. On the other hand, I could have saved a lot of money by having a mentor coach me to conduct more in-depth market analysis and execute with better-defined due diligence.

Find out the median income of homeowners by zip code. Quite a few websites cover this very well, so you should be able to extract the data you need. In addition, you should know the current median sales price of a single family home by neighborhood. You can find this price by looking at many different websites, but the most accurate numbers will come from the local board of realtors.

Know the rental rates and rental vacancy rates for the neighborhood and type of housing (homes, apartments, trailers, etc.) you will be investing in. You can get these from local property managers who work those areas.

You should look at the unemployment rates for the past five years and projected rates for the next two years. I look for diversity in the type of vertical markets that support the area's job outlook. I also look at the percentage of military members in the area because turnover of personnel helps to keep the market steady. Service members receive housing allowance support, which allows them to continue renting and leads to a lot of real estate sales because the service members can also receive Veterans Administration (VA) loans.

The best way to know your market is actually to get your real estate license in that area. Then you will have access to almost all the data you need to make property decisions and you can find a broker to help oversee your contracts. If you choose to work with real estate agents, I recommend you work with those who are active investors themselves. If you don't get your real estate license, your best bet is your local real estate investors club, consulting with a title and escrow team, or driving around the neighborhood and talking to rehabbers and contractors working the area.

Know your market. Create a market analysis and keep it updated annually when new data is released for the city, zip code, or county where you are working. Your market analysis will be your key support tool for deciding on your purchase, rental, and sales. You'll soon become an authority on the area yourself.

Building Your Business Plan

We previously discussed outlining your business plan. Now we need to address how to build it. I always think of my business plan, which I rewrite every year, as a work in progress. Just building the business plan and putting all the parts together helped me to create a better vision of just what my investment business was all about. I am going to share a basic outline that I recommend you use to build a plan so you can establish your own Limited Liability Company (LLC).

I would like to state upfront that you should not overdo your business plan or in-depth marketing analyses. They will evolve, even professionally, over time. The smartest way to spend your time right now is to find buyers and sellers.

Getting started as a real estate investor means collecting information and building relationships that will help you understand how things work, what the possibilities are, and what type of investor you want to become. Once you have most of that information, you should develop a business strategy. Writing out a strategy can be as simple as an outline or a list of bullet statements that define what you intend to accomplish. Don't overwork this. Make it simple and direct. You can hang more meat on this skeleton later. Your strategy and plan will change. Here's an example:

Joshua Smith REI, LLC will purchase properties in the Dayton, Ohio area and rent them out to build passive income.

- *Buy two properties this year for $25,000 to $35,000 using cash from my savings*

- *Budget up to $5,000 for initial rehab work for each property*

- *Use property manager to rent for $600 to $750 per month*

- *Establish recurring costs for taxes, insurance, maintenance, and vacancy rates*

- *Buy two additional properties every following year using loans*

That is very simplified, but it gives you a basic strategy to determine how you want to set up your business, and it has enough objective criteria that you can follow the progress. As a new investor, this plan is enough to get you started with appropriate information to outline your business plan as we discussed in the previous chapter. If you didn't fill in the outline already, let's begin now. I'll give you a brief statement of what each is for and you fill in your own words.

- **Mission Statement:** Should be short and to the point about *what you do* while your vision statement and goals reflect *what you will become.*

- **Goals:** A *state* you wish to be in as a result of this plan such as making enough cash flow to quit your day job.

- **Financial Status:** Used to delineate your assets and liabilities. You must claim the amount of funding you start with, your initial startup costs, expected recurring overhead expenses, the cost and profit rationale you will use on your deals, the sources of your funds, and the distribution of your profits.

- **Target Market Analysis:** The goal is to reveal potentiality of deals by analyzing the demographics of money, people, housing needs projections, unemployment, and new developments.

- **Acquisitions:** You may want to include a breakeven analysis and a summary of profits and losses so you are aware of when you think you'll start making money.

- **Team Members:** List your partners, full-time and part-time, who will be helping you with your purchases, sales, and general business operations.

- **Exit Strategies:** This area includes the methods you may use when selling a property. You might be using seller-financing, a realtor, a 1031 exchange, or—my favorite—a lease-option.

- **Back-Up Plans:** Since there is virtually no deal that will go 100 percent as expected, you should have plans on how to terminate, transfer, or move a property quickly when something goes wrong.

- **Sample Deals:** Break out one or two sample deals so you have a template or checklist that keeps you prepared to analyze a deal quickly.

Don't worry about the size of your first business plan. Focus on including all of the elements you must consider to get the business going. Your plan will grow over time and is postured for a major expansion if you need to present to a group of investors or bankers for the specific backing you might need.

Assembling Your Team

As an investor, you can't do everything all by yourself. Rather, you will be needing a very diversified team of professionals, advisors, and maybe even partners. The bottom line is you need to put the pieces and the players into the combination to make the best deal. Our lives are dyed by the color of our relationships, and you'll need a rainbow of associates to assist you along the way. In this instance, a team is not about hiring folks to work for you; it's more about paying specialists to do their portion of the overall task at hand. Contractors and subcontractors are all a part of your team, and if you make them feel that, they will perform better than you might have expected.

My wife and I are always a team; it's one of those grand things that make a relationship meaningful and inspiring. One of my fundamental rules for building a team is simply that if both of us are good at the same thing—then one of us is not needed. So my wife has become the CIO of our business and I have become the CEO. She's exceptionally good as a "people person," so she assumed the role as the Chief *"Inspiration"* Officer—which leaves me as the incumbent Chief *"Everything Else"* Officer. Yet her role is so much more important than mine. If we cannot inspire people enough to get the business, then we cannot do "everything else." If we cannot communicate pleasantly and professionally, then we risk the deal, the relationship, and our money. She is the better part of the team, and every member she talks to and brings into the deal knows exactly what he or she is getting into.

You will probably have some team members who will be permanent on your team and others who are only on your team when needed for a specific deal. You should, however, build relationships with groups from the following list so you can call on them when you have a deal:

- **Mentor:** Use a mentor early on. We will talk more about having a mentor or being a mentor yourself in Chapter 12. But for now, please understand I highly recommend you have a mentor, or at least a coach, for your first few deals.

- **Deal Hunters:** Get help finding deals. Your immediate resource for deals will be other investors who are involved with your local real estate investors club. They have deals and they have contacts. Look into those deals to find out whether that acquisition type and price tag works for you.

- **Accountant:** You can be your own accountant if you choose. Once you have a few properties, however, you should consider using a tax planner. By that, I means someone who can analyze the impact of deals for current considerations and in the future. It is important because an accountant can discuss depreciation methods, capital gains, and depreciation paybacks. Planning your taxes is probably more important than paying your taxes. (Of course, Uncle Sam won't agree with me on that one.)

- **Insurance Agent:** You must have an insurance agent who understands your business and can get you coverage ASAP for your deals. Shop for rates and pay attention to different insurance agencies' styles of customer service. Generally, when you need insurance on one of your properties, you should expect immediate response and support.

- **Escrow Company:** Learn to work personally with a top-notch title and escrow company. I work with one exclusive escrow officer for each metro area in which I work. She is my choice because she responds quickly and swiftly provides info on liens, taxes, and titles. She also provides options, knows how to close quickly, and helps me with specificity in my contracts for purchase or sale.

- **Property Manager:** You may need the use of a property manager. I did at one time, but now I manage all my properties without those services. Initially, you may be concerned about the 8 or 10 percent they charge for their services, but over time, you will come to realize how much headache they save you. I actually started my own property management company when I grew to thirty properties in one metropolitan area. I got an inside view on how challenging that business is and how very hard it is to maintain a profit while running one.

- **Lender (Banker):** You will need a lender or banker who understands the uniqueness of your business and can help you on both the buy side as well as the sell side. Although you want the best rates, loyalty here can save you a lot in the long run. I also use the same lender to qualify potential buyers. Keeping your partners happy is key to long-term support.

- **Lawyer:** There will be a point in time when you will be standing next to a lawyer in this business. Hopefully, that first occurrence is not in a courtroom. The earlier in your business you begin to work with a real estate attorney, the safer you are going to be.

- **Contractor:** A good contractor may seem like the most challenging team member to get on board, but he or she might also be the most valuable. This team member can cost or save you the largest amount of money in your business. Most investors either do a lot of the work themselves or they hire non-licensed workers to cut expenses. That's how I got started, and I can't tell you how much money I spent because of poor workmanship, needing to redo the job, and actually being swindled.

- **Handymen:** A few good handymen will save you tons of money that you might have otherwise had to pay a general contractor. Little jobs and quick fixes are always needed in this business. If you can find a handyman who has either a plumber's license or an electrician's license, that would be best because you always want to say the work was done by a licensed professional. Having said that, you'll need some lower paid people who can get in and do a job quickly for you in many cases.

- **Local Realtor:** You can use a local realtor to help you buy homes, and possibly for property management, but it's un-likely you will use one to sell. Realtors usually know more about the area than just about anyone else, are familiar with the laws and newer developments, and will be able to get you referrals.

The point of assembling a team of full-time and part-time members is to have all the elements necessary to make your business successful. You want workers who understand your business and can consistently produce reliable results. The best place to outline whom your team members are is in your business plan. Remember the business plan is a living document. It must change as your business, partners, and team members change.

Analysis Paralysis

Many new investors get so involved with analyzing deals that they tend to miss out on some great ones; too often, they weigh-in considerations that keep them from making a deal that matches their business strategy. Quite frankly, it is easy to get stuck by over-analyzing. What I've found is that the intention of analysis is real, but the purpose behind it is nothing more than the fear of getting into a bad deal.

The best way to get over the fear of a deal is quite simply just to do one. You could partner with another investor, or you could use a coach or mentor to guide you through the transaction. The fear will subside the more you do similar deals. I tell new investors over and over, "*Don't wait to buy real estate. Buy real estate and wait.*" Get your feet on the ground by making a real estate purchase and renting it out by using a reputable property manager. This is not a field trip. It is an internship. It is on the job training (OJT). Learning from a book or a seminar will make you think. Learning by doing will make you experienced.

If you are using a mentor, and I hope you are, the numbers are pretty obvious. If you do the numbers on your own, there's no telling what you're going to add in or leave out, while believing you have a sophisticated model with more accurate analytical data than anyone else ever had. I have found that the best way to overcome analysis paralysis is to put a template or checklist in your business plan and use it over and over to look at a deal. If you change the template, and you will, change it in your business plan.

If you find you're still spending too much time analyzing deals to the point of paralyzing your decision-making and execution, think about some of these ideas:

- It is usually the simplest solution that is the best route to success.

- Focus on getting started—not on the final status.

- Give up your belief that the deal will be perfect.

- Set up milestones and objectives to follow.

- You will never be ready to get started—so get started.

Per your business plan, focus first on only one area of investing and become an expert in it. The more deals you make, the more you will learn to cut costs, cut time, and cut risks. Those are the little things you do to grow into an expert. And people love to work with experts. They will pay you to learn how you became an expert. People with money will want to partner with you. People will want to go to your seminar. They will want to read your book and go on your real estate buying tours. And as a result, you will be helping to make others rich while doing the same for yourself.

Developing a Brand—or Developing Brand "A"

What is a brand? Is it your logo? Is it a slogan? Is it a product? The answer is yes. A brand is made up of all of those things, but it's not any of those things by themselves. Basically, your brand is who you are, or your identity. If you consider some of the best-known brands in the world, then you realize that they contain all of those things. Your brand is how people identify you and your business, which means it's not so much the message you send out, but rather it's the message that the customers receive about you. Therefore, brand development is vital to any company. Without the right branding, consumers will choose your identity for you.

It does not matter what kinds of products you sell or how long you've been in business; your business plan needs to include brand development and design. So just why is your brand so important? Because your brand describes who you are and what you're about to your potential customers. The right branding messages plays a key role in many aspects of your company, including determining:

- How your customers recognize and distinguish you

- How you develop your relationships with your customers

- Standard operating procedures, including vision, values, and company maxims

- Your relationships with your employees

Of course, an important part of any brand and brand development strategy is your logo. Your logo can say many things about you. In fact, sometimes, a logo has so much power that it can say just about everything about you, without saying a word at all. Your logo is a visual representation of your brand, and as such, it needs to represent your brand properly. Your logo not only needs to portray your core values to your customers, but it should also be powerful enough that your customers remember those values. Because your logo is so important, you need to make sure it's designed to stand out from the crowd, as well as draw a crowd.

Another important part of brand development is brand-utilizing discovery sessions. These are designed to help you create the right plan for developing your brand. In these sessions, you can sit down with all the necessary players together and discuss what's important to your company and, in turn, what branding messages you want to convey to your customers. In these discussions, you can hammer out your company mission, your core values, and the main purpose of your business that you want to portray.

When it comes to building a brand, it's always a good idea to get some input from the people who will matter the most in the long run: your customers. When you're building your brand identity, you need to know what your customers think of you. By doing targeted research, you can focus on your target market and get its input on your brand, including your logo, marketing messages, values, and how you are perceived. The customer is always right, so listening to others' feedback can play a key role in your brand's success, as well as your bottom line.

There's no doubt that the right branding strategy can go a long way toward creating and maintaining your company's success. That's why following the proper brand development practices is so important. Integrating your marketing and advertising, designing an effective logo, and using targeted research to obtain valuable customer feedback are all part of a successful brand development plan.

Becoming rich is a mindset, much like becoming smart, becoming a writer, or becoming a real estate agent. As with any other aspiration, you *can* become rich!

In some ways, we become what we seek. In full return, what we seek becomes us. Most seek richness in health, wealth, relationships, spiritual understanding, or other things that motivate us to extend ourselves to higher planes of success. Consistent with achieving the American Dream, we also dream of becoming rich.

Summary

In this chapter, we realized that working for yourself can be one of the greatest challenges of your life. You must know your market, have a specific business plan, assemble the right team, and develop a brand that sets you apart from the competition. In the next chapter, we will explore how to grow and maintain your market position using marketing, advertising, prospecting, and sales.

Chapter 7

MAPPING YOUR MARKETING—THE MAPS TECHNIQUE

"The person who stops marketing to save money is like the person who stops a clock to save time."

— Unknown

The one sure thing we know about marketing is that it changes with the times. And if you're going to market your product or services effectively and remain a well-branded entity, you have to establish principles and actions to help you monitor change. Have you noticed that the rules for effective Search Engine Optimization (SEO) change drastically every two or three years? One year, we're building websites; the next, we're blogging. We begin to write articles on LinkedIn, create Facebook business pages, and then we're optimizing keywords and headlines to get more hits. Mobile-friendly content and longer content articles are now the norm. The driving factor is that marketing is all about the user-experience in the users' world.

So do we really care about marketing and advertising as real estate investors? Well, if you consider that the most important thing you sell is yourself, I can think of no group that needs to market itself so much. You must *be known* for something if others are going to remember you when a deal comes up or a specific type of property becomes available. You want everyone associated with property sales and rentals to know your niche, your name, your desires, your limits, and your ability to close a deal.

This chapter covers the most important aspect of branding yourself and remaining current in marketing yourself as an investor. The MAPS technique reminds you to be vigilant about Marketing, Advertising, Prospecting, and Selling (MAPS).

Market Yourself

When starting your real estate involvement, you may not realize the importance of getting the word out to others about how unique and profitable it will be for them to do deals with you. A business is successful only when you give it some time and put a good effort into marketing, advertising, and prospecting. Granted, you may not have a budget just yet, but getting others to know about you is something you can't afford to ignore.

The best way to market yourself is to present yourself professionally, as a person of integrity and as personable; that is… be easy to work with. If you're going to be the owner of a million-dollar business, then you should look and act like the owner of a million-dollar business. People prefer to work with professionals—so put your best foot forward by maintaining an attractive appearance, remembering your manners, and presenting a respectful manner. Being professional also means being honest about everything you say. Never misrepresent yourself. If there are things about real estate investing that you really know nothing about, then share that and use it as leverage to learn from the new person you just met.

Marketing yourself is simply communicating why someone would want to interact with you. Real estate is a personal business, and most investors are usually willing to help a new investor get started, plus they are always looking for a new angle. But they are not looking for people who misrepresent themselves or appear unprofessional or difficult to work with. When you are attending meetings and networking events, you are in the spotlight, so define yourself and your ability to create deals and solve difficult ones. Forget the "elevator speech" hype; tell it like it is—don't sound like you practiced something. Be genuine. Be real. If you have something smart to say, you don't need anything that's memorized.

Show confidence in yourself. No one at your networking

event has been an investor his or her whole life. They all had different jobs before they started investing—just like you. Share who you are, where you came from, and where you're going. You are interesting! You have a story! And people really want to hear it! Now get out there and introduce yourself; shake hands with every person at the event. You didn't go to the event to be quiet, did you? When someone asks how you're doing, tell him what my friend Gary always says, "Today is the best day of my life and you're part of it!" The more positive you are, the more people will remember you.

Don't forget that marketing yourself is not limited to business cards, handshakes, and an elevator speech you gave at your first real estate investors' club meeting. We live in a digital world where we spend more time finding out about one another online than we do meeting and chatting live. People may get an email from you or meet you at a networking event, but most are going to google you as soon as they get home. They're looking for your website, your Facebook page, mutual friends you share, your professional page on LinkedIn, and if you have any blogs or forum comments that they can read to find out more about you. Stay on top of your online reputation and do whatever you can to improve your public image. Here are six smart things you should do to check up on yourself and maintain a positive online image:

1. Google yourself on a regular basis to ensure your image is positive.

2. Develop or update your LinkedIn profile.

3. Make comments about real estate investing in forums, make comments on related blogs, and complete reviews on Amazon books.

4. Remove tags of yourself on unfavorable Facebook photo postings.

5. Make a YouTube video to introduce yourself and explain what you're looking for in a deal. Don't forget that YouTube is the second largest search engine on the planet! You can pretend and mislead people in email, but you can't hide who you really are in video.

6. Establish your ethical clarity by getting an account at www. ethics.net.

7. Set up a Google alert on your name so you immediately get to see anything that is posted. That way you have time to update or delete it before everyone else has access to it.

Did you notice that I said I'd give you six smart ideas, but I actually listed seven? Sorry, but I can't help myself. I live in a world where we always promise good stuff and we always over-deliver. Some things are so important they should be a habit. So this paragraph about recommending to over-deliver is actually smart idea number eight!

Advertising Products and Services

Real estate investors advertise deals, properties, and services. While print media is somewhat expensive, digital services are cheaper and provide greater response. The best service, by far, is Craigslist. You can use it to post properties you want to sell or the types of properties you'd like to buy. You have to keep your ads out front and visible so you will want to post there every single day. Captivating photos get the best responses and the most hits. If you find yourself too busy, you can also use a service such as www.clpvashop.com to post listings for you. The other two online services you might try are backpage.com and eBay Classifieds, but neither comes close to the traffic that Craigslist provides.

Make sure you have a registered account (*my account*) to establish your contact info and password. Once you receive a confirmation email from Craigslist, you're ready to start posting ads. After you have active postings, you can manage them by editing, deleting, reposting, or renewing. This last option, *renewing*, moves your ad back to Top Posting. You can see the status of your ads by color coding:

- Green—active ads

- Blue—ads that you have deleted but you can repost

- Orange—flagged ads that you need to change, delete, or respond to

- Purple—ads that have expired but you can repost

It is important to post in the correct category so you don't receive bad comments or get flagged. Where do you post ads?

Probably in the financial services section or the real estate services section.

On the other hand, you can use Craigslist not only to advertise but also to find deals. There are many FSBOs (For Sale By Owner) and even rental postings that can provide options for you. You should always be on the lookout for owner financing or seller financing, land contracts, and lease options. All you have to do is come together on terms and you can make some quick and simple acquisitions.

You should have about ten favorite sites in your Favorites folder on your computer where you can learn more about advertising prices on corporate websites, forums, and other social media. Here are my top ten, which I keep in a separate folder named "REI Resources." (REI is Real Estate Investing—a commonly used term as you'll see from the website addresses below.)

- NreiOnline.com

- ReiClub.com

- BiggerPockets.com

- CleverInvestor.com

- RichDad.com

- Investopedia.com—Search "Real Estate Investing" for the latest

- Entrepreneur.com—Search "Real Estate Investing" for articles

- Investor.com—If you're looking for venture capital for investing

- Money.Usnews.com/Money

- StrugglingInvestor.Com

There are many others, of course, but you must have *your* favorites for searching information about your business. You may even decide, at some point, to build your own website. Will it bring you a lot of direct business? Probably not, but it will give you an online presence and show your professional side when someone googles you. It will also provide a base where you can advertise and use your own blogs and forums. Then you can use a variety of search engine optimization (SEO) tools to ensure your information shows up on search engines.

Whichever way you decide, you must have a definitive strategy that you can manage and use consistently. As advertising professor Jef I. Richards said, "Creativity without strategy is called 'art.' Creativity with strategy is called 'Advertising.'"

You can build your brand online in so many ways. Many, many groups exist on Facebook dedicated to real estate investors. Facebook also provides opportunities to build your business page and advertise using pay per click. You can also use Shopify to build your online business on Facebook.

Don't forget to use LinkedIn for building your investment awareness and profile online. It has so many forums that you almost have to specify a niche if you are going to read and partici-pate with other like-minded investors.

The opportunities on Craigslist, Facebook, and LinkedIn are incredible. You can get involved with deals, learn about invest-ing, and build relationships as you grow. Use them all for market-ing and advertising. You can also use them for prospecting.

Prospecting Is Key

Before we discuss best practices for prospecting, let's de-fine our target audience. As investors, we need a host of prospects who wear different hats. We need buyers, sellers, financiers, and other investors, just to name a few. We find new prospects using phone calls, texting, email, forums, bulletin boards, direct mail, and networking events.

My first venture in prospecting was my *feet on the street* campaign where I would follow around contractors to find deals and contact the investors who had hired them to do jobs. Contractors get work all over town so they know what's shaking, what's moving, and who's doing the deals. On one occasion, I actually collaborated with two rehabbers to fix up a distressed property and split the prof-its on the sale. This was an easy deal for collaborative effort because I had a buyer before I bought the property. Having an exit strategy before you buy makes it easier to get in contact with your rehabber and ensure the terms are known upfront. If you want leads on buyers and sellers, rehabbers are a key component to prospecting for deals.

Prospecting, as an investor, can be much like prospecting is for a real estate agent. Set a scheduled time of day and a location you are comfortable in and begin your calls. You already know numerous people, and there are others you've never met or had little dialogue with. The people you already know are actually your best avenue for prospecting. Remember to work your sphere of influence consistently for referrals, leads, and prospects.

Begin by calling all the prospects you can get. When you speak to them, be easy to talk to. If you need to leave a voicemail, leave a pleasant message that will make them want to return your call. The most important part of prospecting in the digital age is that you want to stay in touch with your prospects but never be pushy. Staying in touch with them until they are ready to work with you is easy because you can send occasional email with current and relevant information, invite them to webinars, distribute monthly newsletters, etc.

Mail is another way of finding prospects. You can send an email to all the people on your contact list, telling them all about your investment deals, or you can send direct mail to those you don't know to find leads. According to current statistics, the average number of emails people receive per day is about 215, and the expectation is that by 2018, it will be over 225. Many entrepreneurs and larger companies still use direct mail, but even direct mail "ain't what it used to be." Because 90 percent of mail received is trashed without being opened, corporations have engineered better ways at less expense to get buyers' attention.

The total number of presorted, stamped postcards has dropped consistently from 5.8 billion pieces in 2006 to barely 3.0 billion in 2015. Total first class mail has dropped from about 98 billion in 2006 to 62 billion in 2015. There was no one major change in a single year of that time period. It just consistently declines year after year. If you must send direct mail, be sure to make your message meaningful and eye-catching. Using official-looking envelopes will tend to get them opened. Mail that contains items of value, such as coupons, sales, garden seeds, etc. has the best chance of being opened and or kept by the recipient. Write or include something people won't be quick to put in the trash.

Social media marketing is not necessarily the best way to prospect even in this era of advanced technology. You could create a social media page and put all your real estate investing interests there, but you'd have to adopt some Search Engine Optimization assistance if you are going to be seen. Although marketing yourself and advertising your involvements can be used this way, prospecting remains an area in business that works best one on one.

Selling Is Easy with a MAP

I refer here to the acronym MAP because using the MAP techniques will provide continued wealth-building opportunities for you. They will keep you from becoming irrelevant, unknown, or forgotten. All of the above-mentioned strategies for Marketing, Advertising, and Prospecting will help you to reach a broad audience and stay relevant and current. People need to know who you are and what you stand for, and they need to hear from you. You must use these strategies every day. This will promote your business so it will grow more rapidly.

Good branding is what will set your company or yourself apart from others. Branding is usually achieved by having a distinct value in the eyes of those you want to influence. In today's highly competitive world, one must develop and maintain a strong, valuable, and reliable personality or value proposition in order to be successful. Your personality or value proposition is your brand, so it needs to be compelling.

A "value proposition" is a uniqueness that answers the following questions:

- What product or service is your company selling?

- What is the product or service's benefit to the consumer?

- Who is the target group it addresses?

- How is it different from what the competition is offering?

- What do you do to exceed expectations?

For example, a fictional company called Account It Right is selling an accounting app designed to work consistently on personal computers, iPads, and cellphones. It is targeted for small businesses that need quick access, simple input, and error checking during input. It is different because it does not require a CPA and requires almost no training. It also goes beyond expectations by providing a free online chat to a help desk managed by the developer.

Most people don't realize the importance of having and maintaining a distinct brand and how it can tremendously boost their personal success or that of their company. Branding your personality or your company ensures your customers and other people see you the way you want to be viewed. It puts the attention or focus on your personality or your company. It sets you or your company aside from others competitors. It is extremely important to build your personal brand and promote yourself or your company with passion, loyalty, and credibility to make the difference with others. Standing out from the crowd does not depend solely on having a high value proposition, but also on your ability to build and maintain influence over people.

You also need a compelling brand to maintain your and your company's reputation. It is interesting to see how many people and companies have their reputations damaged by powerful and consistent competitors. Most often, this results from negligence or a lack of knowledge on the proper ways to build, manage, and protect one's brand. For personal branding that will make you stand out from the crowd, you must cultivate and develop an unshakable sense of confidence, self-worth, and self-respect. It is extremely important that you be strongly rooted in a clear vision of yourself.

Your brand and core values must be unique and seen that

way. No one will do or say anything to you that is not in direct reflection of how you feel about or present yourself. People will treat you the way you demand to be treated. Your personal brand must reflect what you believe in or stand for to your audience. It shows your audience the value you are presenting. A company must develop unique branding patterns that will become engraved in the minds of past, current, and potential customers. Customers always reward companies that add value to their lives. Your brand's success is in direct proportion to the satisfaction level you bring to your customers' lives. Your personal brand represents your reputation; therefore, it must be maintained and protected properly.

Consistency is a key factor in branding success. Creating a brand and not consistently maintaining it will not do you or your company any good.

Your brand must also maintain the highest quality possible in order to be protected from your competitors. You must consistently and regularly innovate to outpace your competition. Several techniques can be used to manage and promote your reputation. A strong online campaign will ensure that people find and view you the way you want to be viewed. A consistent online search of yourself and your company will ensure that you are aware of how you are viewed by people. It will also allow you to figure out any damage to your reputation so you can respond in a timely manner. Your brand is an extremely valuable asset so you want to make sure it always retains a positive image that stands out from the crowd.

Unless you are the only one in the world to provide a service or product, you are going to face a major challenge from aggressive competition. In almost every business, customers demand high quality and satisfaction, and they have a plethora of choices. So how are you going to make sure your business stays alive in such a jungle? That's where branding become necessary. Sometimes, your brand can be the single most important asset to keep your company running for years. Your product and its quality may be the same as that of your competitors, but you can still make it stand out in the eyes of your customers because of its brand name.

Customers will often even place a higher value on the brand than the product itself. That's why it is extremely important to associate your product with a good brand. Not only will it help your immediate success, but it will help you gain the loyalty of many satisfied customers. Your branding should make it clear why your customers should choose you instead of your competitors. And your attitude toward your customers will help build and strengthen your company's brand further.

Creating a successful brand can be the most important and challenging of your marketing tasks. To begin, you must develop a strategy for linking your brand to your fundamental values. Follow these steps to create a successful value-based brand:

- Name and position your brand to distinguish it from other companies offering the same product or service. Define your brand so it is easily recognizable to customers.

- Look at other companies or businesses offering the same service as yours. What can you do differently that will set you apart and increase your credibility over your competitors?

- Find ways to increase value to your customers. Increased value will keep customers satisfied so they will continue buying from you instead of your competitors.

- Build long-term relationships by offering incentives to your customers. Keep a list of past customers. Reach out to them from time to time, no matter whether you are offering them new products or you just want to make sure they are satisfied with your service.

- Create a unique and compelling logo for your business. It is easy today to have an excellent logo for a small amount of money. Don't downplay having it. It will unequivocally set you aside.

- Use images and a consistent writing style to brand your product. This step is fairly easy to do yourself, or you can outsource through a place like Fiverr or Elance.

- Develop a creative brief that will state your core value. It should be in accordance with the quality of your product or service. Believe it or not, customers will reward or punish you based on the performance of your product or service. They will write reviews about their experiences, and it is hard today to find customers who do not look for a review before making a purchase. So make sure your customers are satisfied.

- Create a direct, decisive, and consistent communication plan with your current and potential customers. Whenever possible, look for ways to talk to your past customers. This should be fairly easy to do in today's digital era.

- Promote your brand in digital and social channels. Have a strong social presence in order to position your brand. Write meaningful and memorable notes to your audience. Research your market to see which social media sites your current and potential customers are using in order to target them better.

- Legally spy on your competitors and possibly steal their clients by offering better services.

- Develop a feedback collection system so you can monitor customer satisfaction. Offer replacements or refunds if necessary to avoid negative connotations. Ask whether there is anything wrong with your product. Your logo should always appear in your communication with customers.

- Trademark your brand to make sure nobody steals it. Monitor your brand closely to make sure no one is posing as your business and stealing your clients.

Managing your brand's reputation is the secret and fundamental ingredient for its long-term viability and success. In order to protect your brand and, therefore, your business, you must pay attention to what is being said about it. Often, customers or competitors will write negative reviews about your brand. Whether or not those reviews are accurate, you must act accordingly to protect your brand.

Depending on the level of damage or the potential for it, you can request the services of reputation management companies. They can use a variety of techniques to dilute the negative effects and restore your reputation.

To increase brand awareness, also consider advertising. Take advantage of the variety of different media types available such as newspapers, magazines, radio, TV, and specific Internet sites that are managed through search engine optimization (SEO). Determine which types of advertising will be most beneficial in terms of your potential customers seeing and hearing your ad. Repeated advertising will make your brand familiar to people so they are more likely to use your product or service.

Once you make prospecting a daily priority, all other things will fall in place. Marketing will be easier because the first thing prospects will do is *google* you to see who you are, and since you will have established your brand on the Internet, they will recognize your quality and position in the market. Advertising will be simpler because you have developed a target audience that knows who you are and will be looking to see what you are selling.

Summary

This chapter laid the groundwork for appreciating how important it is to manage your business day to day. All of this work you do is designed to lead you to making a great deal. And all of it is futile if you don't. What I want you to focus on is not the deal itself. You must focus on your MAP (marketing, advertising, and prospecting). If you do that, then the sales will follow. To recap:

Market you or your company.

Advertise your products or services.

Prospect with everyone you meet or want to meet.

Sales come from actively updating your MAP.

Moving on, in the next chapter, we are going to discuss how to monitor your assets, balance the books, and analyze the numbers.

Chapter 8

COVERING YOUR ASSETS WITH AN MBA

"If you don't have time to do it right,
when will you have time to do it over?"

— John Wooden

When you're swimming in the ocean and an eel bites you—that's a moray! In a twisted sort of way, it's not always bad when things get a little fouled up because it's like a reminder that you're not playing it safe or you're not paying attention. And not paying attention—poor management—is the number one reason why businesses fail. You must manage your assets, balance the books, and always know your numbers.

An MBA is typically known as a Master's degree in Business Administration; however, for the purpose of providing a means for covering your assets, the acronym MBA herein stands for.

- Monitoring Your Debits and Credits

- Balancing the Books

- Analyzing the Numbers

Nothing can get you in deep trouble quicker than not using this MBA formula. So let's look at these three items so you will understand how you can keep your business profitable, legal, and in perspective.

Cover Your Assets

You've worked hard to develop your career. You've done it for yourself. You've done it for your family. You've done it for your retirement. And you've done it for your family's future. You haven't done it to become a target of some lawsuit designed to take it all away. But unless you protect your assets, you are a target in today's world of too much litigation and a lack of privacy when it comes to financial data.

A litigation epidemic has spread across this country. Predatory contingent fee lawyers file thousands of lawsuits each day, many of them with little or no merit. However, juries are awarding unrealistically high settlements in many of these cases. Ever-expanding theories of liability continuously fuel this litigation frenzy. Each successful case is a stepping stone for expansion of liability theory. A few decades ago, people would have laughed at smokers suing tobacco companies, but today, it is a reality. The recent recall of the diet drugs Redux and Fen-phen and the pain drug Vioxx have resulted in an explosion of lawyers suing doctors for prescribing what was a government-approved drug.

Also fueling this litigation fever is the modern-day version of the Robin Hood attitude of "Take from the rich and give to the poor." Lawsuits are rarely brought against someone with no assets or no large insurance policy. In determining whether to sue someone, attorneys will often try to determine whether the target of the lawsuit has enough assets to make the lawsuit worthwhile. As I'll discuss below in the section about financial privacy, inexpensive computerized searches can reveal virtually every asset you own. If the potential pay-off is large enough, a lawsuit will be filed.

Insurance is a two-edged sword. It is a necessary component of all financial planning, but large policies can actually attract litigation. Not only do large liability policies attract litigation, but they can provide a false sense of security. In a substantial number of cases, insurance coverage is *not* available to pay the claim due to policy exclusions for items such as punitive damages, intentional acts, discrimination, or sexual harassment. Verdicts have also exceeded the coverage limits of available policies, and insurance companies have even gone broke.

Don't fool yourself by thinking that you will be okay because you won't do anything wrong. You don't personally have to do anything wrong to be held liable for damages. In many cases, the person held liable had nothing to do with causing the alleged harm. For example, business owners can be liable for employee sexual harassment and auto owners can be liable for a teenage driver's accident.

Lastly, rarely does anyone with wealth have a trial by a jury of his or her peers. Successful businessmen and professionals are often able to be excused or find a way to be excused from jury duty. Additionally, they are excluded from juries by attorneys who are trying to "stack the deck" in their client's favor. Take a look at the twelve people surrounding you next time you are at a fast food restaurant and decide whether you want them to decide your financial future.

It's odd how one is "innocent until proven guilty" in a criminal case, but it seems we are always "guilty until proven innocent" in a civil case. There is no shortage to the danger and perils of being sued, and the possibility of being sued has a direct correlation to the excessive availability of private information.

Virtually every financial aspect of your life is currently being tracked, categorized, filed, numbered, referenced, documented, qualified, registered, indexed, recorded, listed, and archived by private and government sources. This information can be retrieved almost instantaneously through computer searches by government officials, attorneys who want to sue you, and many other persons. As if that were not enough, the federal government spends millions of dollars each year on informants. These informants provide information to the IRS, FBI, and other government agencies. Often, these informants are disgruntled ex-employees, spouses, neighbors, or other persons close enough to you to obtain vital information.

The most important way to protect yourself and your business is through asset protection planning. Unless you take proactive steps to protect your wealth, you stand a substantial risk of losing it. For asset protection to work, planning must be done in advance of the event alleged to have caused the liability. Planning and transactions that occur after an event of liability can be considered fraudulent conveyances, and such planning will only compound your liability. In short, asset protection planning is an effective vaccine, but it is not a cure for liability.

Different methods can be used to protect your business. In all of your business and estate planning arrangements, care should be taken to create effective asset protection. You actually need to develop an asset protection mindset. Asset protection is a process, not a solitary act. Every good asset protection structure requires diligent maintenance to ensure its function.

Asset protection is accomplished by segregating personal assets from business assets and then segregating assets from liabilities. This compartmentalizing of assets and liabilities is done with corporations, limited liability companies, domestic trusts, offshore trusts, and combinations of the same. It also usually includes proper insurance coverage.

Explaining all the tools available to protect your assets is well beyond the scope of this short chapter. However, I hope it will make you think about the need for asset protection so you will take active steps to protect your wealth. Asset protection planning needs to be an important part of your financial plan.

In addition to the pure financial aspect of protecting your assets, a significant mental and emotional component exists. This component is the "peace of mind" you receive from knowing you are financially secure. One very easy way to destroy this peace of mind is to get sideways with the IRS. If you intend to protect your assets and your peace of mind adequately, you must be tax compliant.

Often, effective asset protection plans create a perception of hidden assets. This camouflaging of assets should not lead you to think that out of sight means you do not need to pay all applicable taxes. Taking such a position is tax evasion, and it can lead to financial disaster and even criminal prosecution. A properly-functioning asset protection structure will be tax compliant and all applicable taxes will be reported and paid.

The power of the IRS is vast, so it has the ability to break many asset protection devices. Even if the IRS cannot reach all your assets, the process of disputing with it can be mentally and emotionally draining. If you find your asset protection structure under audit or attack by the IRS, you immediately need to retain a qualified tax attorney to represent you.

The wealth predators are prowling. They know who you

are and they know what you own. One slip can lead to a litigation-feeding frenzy. You must protect your wealth or lose it. Develop a defensive mindset in all your financial affairs. Also, protect your peace of mind. Do not slip into the trap of being non-tax compliant. If your wealth is attacked, defend it with the best litigation attorney you can find. Likewise, if your affairs are challenged by the IRS, hire the best tax attorney you can find. Cover your assets! Your bottom line has to be your top priority.

Monitoring Your Debits and Credits

You should always know your credit score, but it is even more important to review your credit report—the long version. It's amazing what can be found in the details, and although it requires little extra work, you must keep your credit report clean by repairing it when something is incorrect.

Utilization of today's advanced technologies requires huge responsibility. Cellular phones and the Internet, considered as some of the softest technologies, can be easily penetrated by fraud and other illegal acts. Aside from the typical personal bank transaction schemes, financial institutions now consider doing transactions over the airwaves and the Internet. Not to mention that most credit and banking companies use advanced technological network backbones and databases for their record archiving and other banking-related works. All of these may sound unreliable, but these documents also pass through tiny wires and invisible air waves in code formats to make them secure. Nevertheless, the extensive security measures that all financial institutions take to protect their clients are not unbreachable. Millions of fraud reports and cases of identity theft are still unsolved every year. As a result, numerous people annually are victims of lost funds from their credit, debit, and bank savings cards. The need for tighter security becomes more important with each passing year. The chances of you becoming the victim of credit card theft or other related crimes can be eliminated or lowered through your responsible usage of these new technologies.

More than your finances and credits, the most important entry in your accounts to protect is your identity. Identity theft poses many problems such as ruining your history, marring the results of background checks, losing millions of dollars on unsolicited transactions, and criminal lawsuits for doing something you actually didn't do. For that reason, securing and monitoring your credit records is extremly important.

First, make sure that all your transactions are secure. When using the Internet to pay bills and buy products, make sure you only make transactions at highly secure sites that allow you to trace your transactions. Never give your credit card number over the phone unless you were the one who originated the transaction. Always make sure your cards are in your possession or sight. When purchasing at a shop, never allow a cashier to carry your card away from your sight. Always check your transaction online after every purchase.

You can also check your line of credit online. With the use of online credit reports or your bank's hotline, you can possibly monitor the movements of your credit card's finances. You can also access online the three major credit information services in the country— Equifax, Experian, and TransUnion. They can help by letting you know how your line of credit has fared for a given period.

Get a credit report at least once every three months. If you find any suspicious activity in your account, report it immediately to your bank or credit card provider and have your card blocked and replaced. Submit a report for possible identity theft to ensure that your personal information will not be used for any criminal activity.

Remember, technologies can make or break your finances, so use and monitor them in your favor.

Balancing the Books

You don't know whether you're making a profit or operating at a loss unless you balance your books, and if you don't know that information, you cannot pay your taxes properly, which will cause even more trouble for you. To know how to balance your books properly, first you need to understand the three variables in the world's simplest formula for balancing the books: Equity = Assets – Liabilities.

Assets are holdings that have an economic value and are expected to yield a benefit or profit. You should be able to prove how you can convert each asset into cash in order to assign value to it. Assets can be assigned a monetary value, but if they return less than expected, they may destroy your ability to reach your projected growth. Examples of assets include properties, land, buildings, business cars, and office equipment. Your business may establish securities, accounts receivable, cash, and prepaid assets in your accounting principles.

Liabilities basically present a future obligation of your business to pay. They occur when expenditures are made to pay for business operations, to acquire business activities, or to purchase additional properties. Examples of liabilities are income taxes, sales and property taxes, insurance, all debts, and accounts payable (money paid to a contractor for products and services).

Equity is the difference left over when you subtract your liabilities from your assets. It is only correct to the degree that you assign the correct assets and liabilities. In other words, if you do not include office equipment as an asset, the difference in your equity will be off just that much.

You must know your numbers (assets, liabilities, and equity) if you are going to make offers. Although many software packagess exist that you can use, the surest way to get started is to use a template and/or a checklist just to ensure you understand the basics. You probably will outsource your accounting to a certified public accountant (CPA) as your business becomes more complicated and significant tax considerations and options arise to maximize your total profits.

Bookkeeping encompasses all the aspects of record-keeping that you provide to your accounting process. You can track your transactions for each debit and credit as they occur, and you can utilize basic double-entry accounting that you likely learned in high school accounting class to document both.

You can manage your books easily if you know your cash position, record every transaction that has a dollar or value amount, file every receipt, know your cash flow, balance your debts and credits, itemize accounts payable and accounts receivable, manage and monitor a profit and loss sheet (P&L), and manage W-2 and 1099-MISC forms. That sounds like a lot, but if you simply add each of these tabs to the Financials Section of your business plan, you can expand each tab as it applies to your specific business.

You can get assistance in this process by contacting your local Small Business Administration (SBA). You may be surprised by just how helpful your SBA can be. You can ask other investors which software packages they use, or you may already be familiar with popular packages such as Quickbooks, Freshbooks, Zoho Books (the simplest to use), Wave Accounting (which is free), or Quicken.

The sooner you set up your assets and liabilities and begin to document all your transactions, the easier it will be to balance your books. You can now analyze business operations by reviewing the numbers. The good news is you don't need to know college calculus to do this. Basic real estate math is pretty much as simple as *business math*. Actually, most of what you need for real estate math was learned in grade school. It's just that you never really had a reason to apply it until you got your own checking account and credit cards. Now, with your real estate investing business, you can take that application up a notch.

Grabbing the Bull by the Horns

We've all heard the term, "Sometimes you need to grab the bull by the horns." What it means is that when we have a big challenge, we need to brace ourselves, get up the courage necessary, and face it head on. Sometimes, that challenge could have the potential to ruin your business, as in the case of a foreclosure, bankruptcy, or other suit brought on you by a difficult tenant. Please understand that just because it's more difficult, it doesn't have to scare you out of business.

Yes, sometimes things go terribly wrong and they are not simple to fix. But do not let that stop you from making smart business decisions—even if the decision is that you have to change your business. No one is above being sued or harassed by people looking to make money off of honest, hardworking investors.

Maintain your sanity because there is always a way out. Don't fold. Persevere. You or your legal team can save your business so you can continue on despite a very bad problem. My claim here is that you must *not* let the situation consume you.

I started my investment years buying condos for passive income, and that worked great at first. But in 2007-2008, all of the latest condos I bought were losing $300 to $600 a month. Believe me, when you're losing almost $2,000 a month, you need to make hard business decisions. When my wife and I grabbed the bull by the horns and faced the nasty situation, we realized we had to make some changes to how we were doing business. We sold some of our condos, losing as much as $30,000 on each one. We decided we could afford to lose capital, but we could not afford to continue negative cash flow. Even if the decision you have to make is hard, the work you must do to correct the ship can be very demanding; you may constantly be questioning your own decision, and the cost may be high, but you are in this for the l-o-n-g run. We recovered and reinvested in lower-priced properties with positive cash flow. Since then, we've never looked back.

One of the great things about being in business for yourself is the freedom to make business choices. It's your money, your time, and your knowledge. You can choose the hours you work, the types of clients you want to attract, the prices you want to charge, and among other things, how far you want to take the enterprise. You can also choose to change your business. Whatever you decide, you want to feel confident, courageous, and positive.

Change can be a little scary, especially if you're taking your business into territory you're not altogether familiar with. That's okay though—a little fear when looked straight in the eye can instantly be transformed into empowerment.

Please don't think I'm being negative in this section. It is, in fact, a positive and realistic statement that you will face some challenges. I don't want you to go off-course. I want you to believe it's possible, even when difficult, to succeed. I want you to develop a mental attitude that no matter what happens, you will pursue your dream.

Many entrepreneurs and real estate investors fear failure, not because of a lack of confidence, but because sometimes you have to risk *everything*. Many entrepreneurs have failed or thought that at some point in their lives they would fail. Yet those who risked it all finally succeeded in larger ways than they ever could have imagined. Arianna Huffington has one of the most endearing comments about entrepreneurs I have ever heard:

> My mother used to tell me, "Failure is not the opposite of success, it's a stepping stone to success." So at some point, I learned not to dread failure. I strongly believe that we are not put on this earth just to accumulate victories and trophies and voice failures; but rather to be whittled and sandpapered down until what's left is who we truly are.

If you're still fearing failure, it's always good to recall those who have failed and still succeeded. Here is just a handful of my favorite successful entrepreneur stories:

- Harland Sanders, tired of trying to sell his fried chicken through small shops and his own gas station, attempted meeting with 1,010 restaurants before one decided to use his secret recipe in 1952. Kentucky Fried Chicken (KFC) was founded when he was sixty-five years old. The Colonel's legendary recipe is now served in over eighty countries and has sold over one billion chicken dinners to date in almost 20,000 franchises.

- Evan Williams developed a podcast platform that was foiled by Apple's introduction of iTunes. What was next for Evan? He co-founded Twitter.

- James Dyson developed 5,126 prototypes of the bag-less vacuum cleaner over a period of fifteen years before he finalized a successful product and introduced the line of Dyson vacuum cleaners.

- Fred Smith entered his business idea as a Yale university student. He received a nearly failing grade but stuck with his idea to open a company based on it. That company is FedEx.

- Vera Wang was a U.S. figure skater who worked her whole life to make it to the Olympics, only to fail to make the Olympic figure skating team. She then used her education to apply for an editor's job with *Vogue* magazine and was turned down. Deciding to pursue her inner love for fashion design, she is known worldwide today for her high-end wedding gowns.

- Milton Hershey was a hard worker who pushed his apprenticeship efforts as a printer to open his own print shop. When that failed, he tried to start three candy companies, which also failed. He finally found acceptance for his chocolates and is now a household name, selling almost $7 billion annually.

- As a single parent who lived on public benefits through years of tragic family losses and hardship, J.K. Rowling had her manuscript, *Harry Potter*, rejected by twelve publishers. She finally had her first book published in 1997 at the age of thirty-two and became the author of the bestselling book series of all time.

- Walt Disney, dismissed by his newspaper editor as having no creativity or imagination, actually went bankrupt several times before he developed his now world-famous Walt Disney studios and amusement parks, worth over $35 billion.

- Oprah Winfrey was fired by her news station in Baltimore, but she went on to leverage the strength of daytime television entertainment to make her worth almost $3 billion today.

- Jeff Bezos established an online auction site, zShops, which failed entirely. Refusing to quit, he transformed his online creativity into the worldwide business known today as Amazon.com.

- Larry Ellison, CEO of Oracle Corporation, co-founded his business with his ex-boss after he dropped out of college and worked in the software business for almost ten years. Larry had to mortgage his own home with a line of credit to keep his fledgling company afloat.

- Henry Ford developed two automobile companies that both failed. His now famous Ford Motor Company, founded on the lessons learned, had a net worth in today's dollars of almost $170 billion at the time of his death in 1947.

- A young wannabe actor was auditioned by Metro Goldwyn Mayer (MGM) in 1933 only to be let go—noting that he was slightly bald and couldn't act or sing. That note hung over the fireplace of Hollywood homeowner and movie star Fred Astaire for many years.

These somewhat superhuman achievements are not just for the lucky ones but for the persistent ones. Such achievements are possible for *you* if you persistently endeavor to achieve success in the pursuit of your dreams. You have as much potential as the most successful CEOs, artists, presidents, and inventors. When you persevere, you will find success beyond your wildest expectations.

Summary

The last four chapters, Section II of this book, built a framework for understanding the business of real estate investing. No matter what kind of business you have, whether it provides products or services, you must apply business management principles or you will find yourself in the throes of failure. The next section is about mentoring. If there is one point I wish to make here, it is twofold:

- If you are new to investing, you really should have a mentor. And if you decide not to, there will come a day when you're going to hear me whispering, "I told you so."

- If you are already a sophisticated investor, you can get more deals and expand your business by being a good mentor to others.

SECTION III

PREPARATION, EDUCATION, and APPLICATION

"Winning is the science of being totally prepared."

— George Allen, Sr.

Whether you are a brand new investor or well-experienced in doing a lot of deals, a time will come when you will have the opportunity to give back. When that opportunity arrives, don't pass on it—even if you know you're not perfect. You can still make a difference helping others, and you will grow in your abilities to help. You may think you don't have enough experience to be a great mentor, but even if you're not polished, you can still shine!

Giving back means helping newer investors get deals that will change their lives and ground them in a business that will allow them to walk away from a W-2 job. Coaching is an accepted pay-for-service that most young entrepreneurs are willing to embrace for their short-term training. I have nothing against coaching as long as the person paying is clear that a coach is there for the money and will probably try to upsell the client at some point. Mentoring is about giving back so that others may move forward. It's an opportunity to get rich by doing things for others that are absolutely priceless.

Probably the most overrated words in real estate investing are "expert" and "guru." Most of the real estate industry is unregulated, so it's almost impossible to enforce rules or hold people responsible for unethical behavior. Some get reported, caught, and fined, but little can be done to ensure that a new investor or homeowner will be working with a professional who can truly help make his or her dreams come true. If an investor mentor is really there to help *you*, she won't be concerned about being *paid*. I know a lot of investors may disagree with that, and I understand that investor mentors are trying to make money too, but if you coach for money, you are not a true mentor.

This section is about how to share your wealth of knowledge with others, how to check in with yourself to ensure you are ready to be a coach or mentor, and how to be results-oriented while helping less-experienced investors grow through this wonderful experience.

Chapter 9

SHARING YOUR WEALTH

"The happiest people in the world are those who have invested their time in others. The unhappiest people in the world are those who wonder how the world is going to make them happy."

— John Maxwell

Mentoring and coaching others is always a priority if you want to help others accomplish their objectives and attain their goals. My hope is that you can take the knowledge and wealth you have learned and earned and turn it into a fortune for others. Those you help to succeed will always be appreciative and, hopefully, they will be inspired to help others in turn. In this chapter, we'll look at some specific qualities and actions you should provide as a mentor or coach.

Those you coach will more readily see and appreciate what you are offering when they sense that you are sharing the wealth with them. That sharing can be in terms of knowledge, skills, time, or engaging them as players in a business deal. The surest way to gain their appreciation is to build trust, help them to define and measure clear objectives, and provide them with active participation in a real estate transaction.

Few business ventures require as great a need for mentoring as real estate investing. The gates are wide open because the opportunities for creative financing and wealth-building are boundless—provided they are within the limits of the law.

This chapter is dedicated to the concepts of sharing your wealth by coaching, which encompasses applying your time and resources in a way that you can make others rich first. I have never charged a fee for mentoring, so I hope you will be equally generous. The benefit of making others rich first is that I get rich in the process—in so many ways.

Why Everyone Needs a Business Coach

Everyone has heard the term "business coach." Do an Internet search on Google, MSN, or Yahoo and you will easily get more results than you can ever read. Each coach you find will say he or she can help you and your business, but what can a coach really do for you? And most importantly, why do you need a business coach? There are seven reasons.

Seven Major Reasons Why You Need a Business Coach

1. To make more profit

2. To provide direction in marketing and selling your products

3. To keep you accountable

4. To fast-track your success as a business owner

5. To have an experienced shoulder to bounce ideas off

6. To hold your hand in the step-by-step process of growing your business

7. To help you find the right people for your organization

Let's look at each of these reasons in more detail.

1. **To Make More Profit:** Have you been in business for a few years now, but your business has grown stagnant? Are you making enough profit to get by, but you're not really going anywhere? A business coach will teach you how to turn your business around and take it to the next level. What a business coach will teach you will apply not just to one business, but to all your businesses. You can apply the principles you learn to any business you own.

2. **To Provide Direction in Marketing and Selling Your Products.** You have the perfect product, but even with advertising and marketing, nothing is happening. So do you give

up? No. Instead, hire a business coach who is an expert in your field and who will be reliable in helping you. A business coach will show you how to market your product and how to find the right target market. With the right audience, you can market your products and/or services correctly. Once you understand proper marketing procedures, you can apply them in the future to anything you wish to sell.

3. **To Keep You Accountable.** A business coach will keep you accountable for your business and what you should be doing to grow your business. He or she will be there to guide you each step of the way, while you put what you learn into practice. The coach will not do it for you, however. You will learn by doing it hands-on. What you learn can then be applied to any marketing campaign, now and in the future.

4. **To Fast-Track Your Success as a Business Owner.** Just like a talented athlete has a coach, you would use a business coach to give you structure and guidance through the learning process of running a business. A business coach will put you on track and show you what to do at the right times. He or she is your coach, mentor, consultant, and advisor. He wants to make your business the best it can be—a world class champion business.

5. **To Have an Experienced Shoulder to Bounce Ideas Off.** It can be lonely running your own business. You need someone who can answer your questions on all parts of your business and who will let you bounce ideas off him, as well

as give you instructions and help you look outside the box to gain a different perspective. A business coach is like a silent partner. A partner who has a financial interest in the business, but lets you keep the rewards.

6. **To Hold Your Hand in the Step-By-Step Process of Growing Your Business.** Sometimes in business, you get to the point where you are a bit unsure of what to do next. You feel like you want to hit your head against a brick wall. A business coach will give you guidance on the next steps you need to take to prepare things and what you need to do when you are doing it so it will be more comfortable for you. A business coach is like a guardian angel. He or she is there for you every step of the way, guiding you with a helping hand.

7. **To Help You Find the Right People for Your Organization.** A business coach will help you find the right people for you and your business. He will let you know the secrets of the correct way to attract and recruit the right people. You can use a recruitment agency, but it will hire the person it thinks suitable. And generally, that person will not be ideal. A business coach will help you find the perfect person.

Giving Your Knowledge, Time, and Money to Others

Allowing people some space for action within your organization will power its fast growth because everybody will be effective and engaged. Make people mini-entrepreneurs so they enjoy the benefits of success. These newly-molded entrepreneurs will watch your back and propel revenue. Furthermore, take advantage of techniques to share wealth with others and, of course, experience growth. Some of these techniques include:

- **Top to Bottom:** Making sure all share in the riches from the least paid to the top men

- **Quality Is Critical:** Making sure you have great services that entice clients

- **Black and White:** Making the targets clear and objective

- **Big Money—Big Motivation:** The more money someone makes, the more he or she is motivated

In the sharing of wealth, giving time and money is so essential. Although the literature on volunteering behavior and health is relatively well-established, intriguing work also finds correlations between making charitable donations and psychological wellbeing. These correlations are consistent across many different cultures. What remains to be seen is whether giving to others makes people happier, happier people simply give more, or some third variable exists to explains this finding.

The majority of studies on volunteering are focused on older adults, yet volunteering appears to have a beneficial effect on other populations as well, including younger adults with post-traumatic stress disorder (better treatment outcomes). In both correlational and longitudinal studies, volunteers report more positive effects, greater life satisfaction, and enhanced psychological wellbeing, and less depression compared to non-volunteers, even when considering a variety of covariates. Evidence seems to exist for a curvilinear effect of volunteering that shows there are mental health benefits associated with moderate levels of volunteering, but not extremely high levels.

Volunteers who donate their time for other reasons (e.g., out of compassion) experience a significant reduction in their mortality risk, but volunteering for more self-oriented reasons (e.g., to learn something new, or to feel good about oneself) is not associated with any change in mortality risk. In fact, after considering covariates, self-oriented volunteers are just as likely to die as older adults who do not volunteer! Although volunteering behavior itself appears to enhance or sustain mental and physical health, there are inconsistencies regarding how much the type, number of organizations, duration, or frequency of volunteering matters, with some research suggesting that these factors play no role and others finding that they do matter. A meta-analytic integration of the literature would clarify this, and indeed, researchers are working on exactly this issue.

Measures of social support given encompass both practical support (e.g., time, knowledge, money) and more emotional types of support (e.g., listening to and encouraging friends and family). Several correlational studies find that giving social support to others is associated with higher psychological wellbeing, including increased happiness, raised self-esteem, and less loneliness. These findings are confirmed in longitudinal studies.

Experimental and quasi-experimental studies find that people who are randomly assigned to such behaviors as caring for plants, giving money to others, or sharing from their reservoirs of knowledge experience increased psychological wellbeing and decreased depression. However, giving is not always related to more positive *mental health* outcomes. One study found no relationship between giving social support and depression, and some studies have revealed that giving social support can sometimes be associated with negative outcomes such as a sense of burden and frustration, especially if others make too many demands, if givers become overwhelmed by others' problems, or if there is low reciprocity within the interactions.

Growth through Giving

Reward yourself by giving of your time, knowledge, and money to others. Big benefits can result from giving of your time; helping others can actually make you feel like you have more time to yourself, for real. It is a known fact, tested and trusted, that people who spend time helping others feel less time-constrained and better able to complete their myriad of tasks and responsibilities. Whether you donate money or time, giving back is beneficial—and not just for the recipients. Research has shown that the old adage, "It's better to give than to receive" is true after all.

Giving of your time and money allows you to make social connections, give back to the community, develop and grow as a person, gain a new perspective about life, boost your self-esteem, and know that you are needed. (Feeling needed and appreciated is important for one's wellbeing.)

Once you start giving, keep giving. The faster you give money away, the more money will flow back to you. Not because of karma or universal cosmic forces, but because you then spend less time defending it and more time making more of it. Investing in private companies you think can do well is another sensible way to stay rich, but giving it away on a continual basis is a surer route. By the way, when you do start giving it away, find someone to do it for you. Most of my money is given away by a lovely lady accountant called Catherine Bishop, and she does a far better job of it than I.

As soon as you've spent it, gifted it, loaned it, or invested it, forget about it. More angst and worry comes into the world from concern over past investments, loans, or gifts than can be imagined. It's gone, so forget about it. If any of it returns to you, fine. But that should not be your primary concern, unless you invested for safety's sake, which is a different matter. Do not waste time playing the blame game over investments, loans, or outright gifts, however large. The blame, if there is any, is yours.

Never loan money to friends. If you loan money to a friend, you may lose your friend as well as your money. Give your friend whatever you feel like giving. Then forget it. Ditto with relatives. If you diligently follow this one piece of advice, you will be saved a sack full of misery. Trust me. Broadcast your policy loudly. This will spare you from many embarrassing demands that will otherwise vex you.

Studies show that our giving behavior rewards us in positive ways. There are a variety of reasons why growth comes through giving. Here are a few of them:

- Giving to others helps us feel that we have efficacy and agency, which essentially means that when we realize we are making a difference in someone's life, it feels good to us.

- Charitable works provide meaning and purpose to our lives. By helping others, we truly help ourselves by making us feel we have a purpose, a mission, a calling, and that our efforts matter to others. If our efforts matter, then we matter.

- Social comparisons: Being around those who struggle more than we do—financially or otherwise—makes us feel better about our own situations. Hopefully, we don't feel superior to those less fortunate, but we do feel smart, wealthy, or generous when we are around those who do not share our good fortune.

- Our society is anchored by various faiths, and all of them have traditions of encouraging their congregations to help others for moral and religious reasons. At the end of the famous Good Samaritan parable in the Gospel of Luke, Jesus states, "Go and do likewise."

- Giving to others is adaptive in community living. As social animals, we survive as a species when we cooperate with others and care for those in need. Thus, from an evolutionary and socio-biological perspective, we are wired to help others within our community, and doing so helps all of us survive and thrive.

Making Others Rich First

My world changed when I bought my first home. It changed because of all that I learned so quickly from the loan process, the escrow process, the legal documents I had to sign, and from taking a more critical look at my personal data—data I had never paid particularly close attention to before was now upfront and center for the first time. Those things included my credit review, debt to income analysis, tax deductions, and loan to value ratio of the property. Those, and a number of other things, made me view my money and my future wealth at a much higher level.

After reviewing all of this and realizing how easy it is to understand, I couldn't help but ask myself why I had never done it before. Why had I never taken a long, interested view of my wealth and my opportunities to build it? The primary reason is that you really have to be *ready* to buy a home. It has to fit your lifestyle. People wait for numerous reasons; similarly, they have reasons why they wait to become interested in building wealth. The more I read about how to build wealth and discuss it with others, the more I realized how many times in my past I could have been building wealth—even without having bought a home (although I consider that the smartest thing to do to build wealth).

I believe there are three major reasons why most American fail to get very wealthy:

1. They overpay their taxes.

2. They fail to save 10 percent of their income.

3. They fail to put their money to work.

Lack of education or an absence of a desire to know causes most American not to understand the tax laws and provisions that have been established to help us not pay so much in taxes. Oddly, many sneer at the wealthy for knowing how to keep their taxes low, but the insanity is that everyone has these same opportunities. Everyone just hasn't taken the time to learn them, apply them, and seek counsel through a CPA or tax consultant. Please be sure to apply those three principles so you can get started on managing your financial portfolio.

Believe it or not, most Americans pay more in taxes than they need to. There are some basic concepts you can learn so you *don't overpay your taxes.* You can start by reviewing your annual filings and return so you know where you stand. Next, look candidly at the effects you will have reducing your taxable income when you:

-   Have your taxes prepared by a professional

-   Put part of your paycheck into an IRA or 401K plan

- Buy a home or an investment property

- Determine whether you qualify for an Earned Income Credit

- Start your own business

- Create college savings accounts

- Don't pay off your mortgage early

- Give more money to charities and claim it

- Learn which of your medical expenses are tax deductible

- Check for current tax credits using solar or energy-efficient solutions

You must discipline yourself to make saving your money more important than paying your bills. You can do that by making sure you *save 10 percent of your income* from every single paycheck or other transaction that provides you income. Many employers or banks can help you establish an automated deduction to send 10 percent to another account such as a 401K.

What if I told you that if you save 10 percent of your pay, you will actually be making more money?

Okay, now—STOP! Don't read ahead. Just close your eyes and think about how crazy this sounds: If you save 10 percent, you will make more money. I didn't say you'd be saving more money. I am saying you will actually be adding more money into your life that way. That's sounds better than getting a good pay raise! Here is an example to explain how it is possible.

Pay without Deductions

Let's say you make $3,500 per month—and you get paid $1,750 twice a month. And, to make it simple, let's say you pay 35 percent of your salary in Social Security, income tax, etc.

You would end up with $1,137.50 ($1,750 − 35 percent) in your checking account twice a month. The result is an annual take home pay of $27,300 ($1,137.50 x 24) while paying $14,700 ($612.50 x 24) in annual taxes.

Pay with 10 Percent Deduction

Now we'll look at the same pay, but put 10 percent of your pay into a 401k plan.

Deduct 10 percent ($175) and add employer's matching ($175 + 50 percent) and you have $262.50 that goes into your retirement account every two weeks. Your 401K would grow $6,300 a year ($262.50 x 24).

Same as above, you pay 35 percent in Social Security, income tax, etc. But in this case, you are paying less your 10 percent for taxes: $1,750 − $175 = $1,575 taxable income.

Taxable income for the year would be $37,800 ($1,575 x 24) so your taxes at 35 percent would be $13,230, which is almost $1,500 less than you'd be paying if you weren't saving your 10 percent.

You would end up with $1,023.75 take home pay twice a

month ($1,750 – $175 = $1,575 and $1,575 – 35 percent = $1,023.75)

So what happens at the end of the year?

	No Deductions	10% Deductions
Annual Salary	$42,000	$42,000
Taxable Income	$42,000	$37,800
Payroll Taxes paid	$14,700	$13,230
Annual Take-Home Pay	$27,300	$24,570
Take home twice a month	**$ 1,137.50**	**$ 1,023.75**
Annual 401K Growth	**$ 0**	**$ 6,300**
Annual Gain	**$27,300**	**$30,870**

Summary:

You gave up 10 percent of your income ($4,200) in take-home pay for one year, yet you have accumulated $6,300 in savings (thanks to employer matching), and you paid $1,470 less in taxes. And you will be filing your income tax forms to pay against $37,800 adjusted gross income instead of against $42,000.

If you add your take-home pay ($1,137.50 x 24) plus your savings ($0), the person with no deductions has a total of $27,300 to show for the year.

The person who did 10 percent deductions ended up with $30,870 ($1,023.75 x 24 = $24,570 + $6,300) to show for the year. The bottom line is always the bottom line: You are deducting $113.75 twice a month but making $3,480 more at the end of the year—a difference in your wealth-building of almost $300 a month!

What would that mean if you did it for thirty years? I won't even bother with a table to reflect the figures because I know you *get the picture*. And there is much more to this picture because of tax deferrals, accelerated mutual funds margins, etc., but what's important is that you see how saving 10 percent is one area where everyone can build wealth.

There are so many other ways to save money each month, and each way will help you pay less taxes—either before you put your money into savings, or by putting money into savings after you pay your taxes (Roth IRA). The important thing is that when you pay yourself each month, you are building wealth.

We have discussed a lot of things you can do to pay less taxes, and we found out that saving 10 percent will allow you to live, work, and retire comfortably. So let's review the third proven wealth principle. Many people have positioned it correctly: "I want to put my money to work so I don't have to work so hard for my money."

Let's face it: The only true way to *put your money to work* is to save a fair amount of money that enables worthwhile growth. The primary reason why is that higher returns come with higher risks, and when you're getting started, you need to be extremely careful where you put your money. Also, lower amounts of capital usually grow less money than a higher amount. There's no way around that without high risk ventures.

Comedian Steve Martin used to do a routine where he explained how easy it is to make a million bucks. "First," he would say, "get a million bucks…." He is absolutely right. If you have $500 and make a 100 percent profit, you'd have made $500. If you have $1,000,000 and you only make half that profit (50 percent), you'd have made $500,000! A lot of people are willing to risk $500 to make a big payoff, but very few are willing to take on a high-risk, million-dollar venture. In a very fair, yet ironic twist, Steve Martin was making millions of dollars telling jokes about how people could make a million dollars. It shows how truly brilliant he really was.

It's pretty common financial advice to have a readily available savings account, but you may not need more than three to six months of cash in it. There are a number of ways to get your cash off the bench and into the game. Here are some ways to put your money to work:

- Create a passive income stream with investment properties.

- Strategize with penny stocks or other stocks that grow year in and year out.

- Put your money into a high yield savings account or money market account.

- Store your money in an IRA or 410K account for growth and tax savings.

- Set up a website for an Internet sales business.

- Become a member of a successful network marketing campaign.

- Get out of debt and use the money you were paying in interest.

- Choose credit cards that provide rewards so your money will be growing.

- Learn how to budget smartly by putting every dollar you have into a category.

- Use the money in your IRA.

As your money begins to provide returns, you should keep reinvesting it in one form or another. My favorite investment is passive-income properties. Let me tell you a story about how I make them work for me.

In April 2010, I bought a property listed for $20,000, but I paid $14,500 cash for it. Over the years, I have put over $15,000 into upgrading it, so let's say $20,000 in rehab. It began renting out for $725 a month in 2010, and it continued to rent up to $900 a month before I finally sold it in August 2016. It was sold on a lease option contract with none of the tenant's rent going toward the settlement price of $68,500. There was no property management involved because the tenant had agreed to first right of purchase, and he took extremely good care of the property because he knew it was going to be his home. I did absorb costs carrying insurance and paying taxes, but there was no other overhead, so putting my $35,000 of cash to work for me produced both passive income for over six years plus a capital gain of over 100 percent. Not all of my deals have worked that well, but if you do your homework, you can find plenty of deals that do as well or better.

It should be no surprise to anyone that we really can't help others get rich until we experience the trials and successes of wealth ourselves. Your firsthand testimony is much more powerful than a seminar, book, or attendance at an investors' club meeting. You will come across to others as believable and as an "If I can do it, so can you" role model. I believe the best way to be the real deal is to take steps to increase your wealth, share your story, and then help others get rich without charging a fee. Before we close this chapter, here is my list of the top ways you can help others get rich first.

Top Ten Ways You Can Help Others Get Rich First

- Show people how to maximize tax-deferred or tax-free retirement accounts.
- Explain how to pay off credit card balances every month.
- Help people set up and acquire investment properties.
- Assist people in developing smart objectives to reach their goals.

- Show others how and where to set up their own LLC for business.

- Explain how refinancing a home mortgage can help build wealth.

- Teach people how and where to become more knowledge-able about tax breaks.

- Live like you're poor so you have more money to work with.

- Show others how to use their money as hard money or private money.

- Provide an education in how money works.

Summary

This chapter was focused on explaining why experienced investors should share their knowledge, time, and money not only to help new investors get started, but to expand their riches by being involved. Now we move on in the next three chapters to explaining the preparation and education needed for mentors and coaches and how they can apply it to help build win-win deals with newer investors.

Chapter 10

PREPARING TO COACH OTHERS— *THE PREPARATION*

*"If you light a lamp for someone, it
will also brighten your path."*

— Buddhist Proverb

Aristotle is a towering figure of ancient Greek philosophy. He studied the arts and sciences under Plato—who was taught directly by Socrates. One of Aristotle's more influential books, *Rhetoric*, defined how to build and maintain persuasion and influence working with others. His basic explanation is that most people are led in their lives by either passion or logic, but a leader must have both the inner drive of passion and the logical assembling of ideas to extend the rhetoric that guides others' decisions.

You may, like me, know these two types of personalities—people who are either driven by their passions or consumed by logic. People can be stuck in decision-making, or they can make decisions too quickly; either situation can dominate and control the direction of their business and relationships.

The three factors that shape a leader are logos, pathos, and ethos. *Logos* (logic) means that you must make sense and be able to explain things logically. *Pathos* (passion) is what must be used to reflect your enthusiasm. A leader must have control of both logic and passion, and utilize the third, *Ethos* (ethics), as the foundation of his or her character that holds logic and passion together.

Similarly, great salesmen display the power of rhetoric when they appeal to our inner passions in such a way that we decide to buy into what they are saying. But many times, because our rational self is not satisfied, we are hesitant to follow their advice and look at them suspiciously. In other instances, we become so overwhelmed by studying the numbers that we tend not to listen to our guts. The balance we seek can be found in a controlling influence that will help us make better decisions; hopefully, we find a mentor who can provide that influence and balance. That mentor will guide us in our decisions and help us build confidence through the actions based on those decisions so we can make the best real estate investing decisions.

This chapter is about preparing yourself for involvement with other real estate investors so you actually help them make the best decisions so they can get rich…first. The student and the teacher both learn through each experience. The following two chapters will build on how best to help others by explaining the necessary education of an experienced real estate investor who wants to be a mentor and how to remain motivated and enthusiastic while also providing constructive feedback and direction to less-experienced investors.

You're not going to be "Alexander the Mentor" by the time you finish reading this chapter, but your awareness of the need for logic, passion, and ethics will help mold your practices into becoming a great mentor. Preparation is where performance begins, and if we revisit why we initially became involved with real estate, we can appreciate the need for a coach or mentor. We can also appreciate why we want to become the mentor that we never had. Preparing to coach means becoming totally involved in the goals and vision of the person you are helping. It requires you to understand the person's time allotted, his or her access to funds, and how much basic investing the person already understands. You can gain influence over others when you make a lot of money doing deals yourself because people love to follow a winner. But you can gain even more influence when you give away what you've learned. That's what a mentor does.

Getting Involved

What first made you get involved in real estate? Was it the money? Was it that crazy feeling in your blood that just got boiling anytime someone started talking about it? Was it because it sounded so good and so easy for anyone to get involved? However it happened, for most of us, it led to the realization, "Hey, I can do that!"

What was your initial motivation for getting more deeply involved with investing? Most people usually reply with one of the following: creating positive cash flow, buying and selling to make a quick buck, getting more tax deductions, or not wanting to stress out about retirement but instead make my money work hard for me so I don't have to work hard for my money.

In all the time I've worked with new investors, I've never met one who is only interested in doing just one single deal. They all seem to have a long-term plan, and it's all about financial freedom.

To achieve any task, you have to be involved as a leader and investor. To create a truly effective performance management process that supports wealth and investment, development and success—your total involvement is of paramount importance.

You were coached when you got started in real estate, and your coaches and mentors learned so much about deals because of their involvement in your success. Because they decided to help you get rich first, they got rich in the process. They became rich by:

- Understanding deals they never would have been involved with

- Making future similar deals

- Learning solutions

- Sponsoring and partnering in similar deals

Coaching others was the tipping point for me in my personal business. Every person I helped make a deal provided me with impactful knowledge for enhancing my own portfolio. Once you have made a deal or two, it's time for you to get rich by making others rich—first. You'll see greater riches than you would have ever believed. The best way to get that rolling is to learn how to be an effective real estate investment coach.

So what makes a good coach, and how can you best prepare for coaching's demands? Coaches usually have a total immersion program rather than teaching in a classroom or at a seminar. You pretty much get your training as a coach through your experiences with making deals. Coaching is about getting the very best out of a trainee and enabling her to make decisions that will improve her situation, which, in this case, happens by investing smartly in real estate. You, like all coaches, will make mistakes, but you'll also have soaring victories. But what makes you most appealing is that you've actually done something a newer investor wants to experience herself.

Having said that, you must develop several skills to use in the coaching process. They include the obvious ones: good communication, knowing how to build positive rapport, providing motivation and inspiration, and commitment to schedules and expectations. Altogether, these skills will convince the person you are coaching to buy in to you. That means you have to be credible, resourceful, responsive, and a guiding light.

Build your own template of the persons you are coaching by finding out or reviewing their goals and helping them write clear measurable objectives. This task alone will help build a path you want to follow. You'll also have to know the availability and limits of their resources—their knowledge, time, and money. Find out from them:

- How much do they know and what do they need to know to do a deal?

- Will they be using their money or someone else's?

- What price level of properties are they looking for?

- How much time each week can they spend working on a deal?

- Are they flippers or seekers of passive income?

- Which locations are they willing to work with?

- How quickly are they looking to get something in place?

Growing Your Interest

The best way to grow your interest as a new investor is to network, join an investors' club, attend seminars, get your real estate license, and help others.

Think back to your own beginnings. Once you were initially motivated, what did you do to grow your interest and involvement? One of the first things you may have done is join a real estate investment club like I did. There are many real estate investment clubs to choose from. Search for a local group at the National Real Estate Investors Association (NREIA) website at http://nationalreia.org/find-a-reia/

It's important to know whether it's a for-profit or non-profit group. Both are legitimate, but they may have attributes that do not favor your growth and development, such as limiting opportunities, charging high dues and fees, pitching for sales, and restricting training opportunities. Either way, you will learn to network with other investors—a wonderful opportunity to have.

Be mindful of for-profit versus non-profit clubs. You can usually tell a for-profit because the club's officers have been the same for many, many years, whereas a non-profit will change leadership every one or two years. My experience has also been that over 75 percent of the people who attend the for-profit groups never actually do a deal or they quit after one or two. Non-profits are preferred because they are much more open to deals and deal making, whereas for-profits tend to control how things are done— as they should since they are in a business themselves.

Attending real estate investment seminars is probably the best way to get fresh perspectives on investing. The genuinely useful seminars are typically organized by serious real estate investment companies, and they provide insight, guidance, materials, and coaching. The speakers at these seminars usually are hugely thriving investors who have amassed great wealth themselves and will inspire you to attain wealth in the same manner they did.

The reality is that only a few of these seminars are genuinely useful because they may not be timely, relevant, or fully disclosing their operations and intentions. I think the word *prey* is a pretty strong word, but I'd say most of these seminars do *take advantage of* those who really don't know which turn to take and are willing to pay money hoping they'll get smart enough to do deals. The majority of speakers will tell the truth about how they made money with a specific method. Unfortunately, the laws, practices, and markets have usually changed so much since then that all you are getting is a testimony instead of an opportunity. It should be well-noted that many get-rich methods that worked a few years ago may not be working today. It may also be difficult to ascertain who the speakers are going to be and what their credentials actually are. The term *expert* is grossly misused in real estate investment circles. When you google the speaker's name, be mindful that some may have loaded their own reviews and, through SEO optimization, made sure their own reviews will come up first instead of those by actual attendees who may have had a different perspective.

If you want to be a full-time real estate investor, you might consider getting your real estate license. You may find, as I have, that there are many incredible deals available that you would have likely never found out about. You will also discover that you'll know the good deals before they even get listed. You will quickly become very knowledgeable about your local real estate market as well as the entire industry on a national basis. A license is required of individuals who conduct licensed real estate activities as described in the Real Estate Law under the supervision of a licensed broker. A license may also be obtained by a person who does not immediately intend to be employed by a broker. A salesperson without an employing broker may not perform acts requiring a real estate license and only be holding an inactive license.

I have found the best way to learn about anything is to take on the responsibility of briefing the topic or teaching it to others. As a matter of fact, as most of us have learned, the best way to learn is to teach. According to the published research studies of Dr. Jon Nestojko in *Memory & Cognition*, "When compared to learners expecting a test, learners expecting to teach recalled more material correctly, they organized their recall more effectively and they had better memory for especially important information." The reason is that the mindset of a teacher is to determine key points of required learning and organize information into a structure he or she can teach from.

I recall one seminar speaker who told me, "I always give the same talk. When I give it for free, everyone says, 'Good job; you're a great speaker.' But if I charge a fee for the same talk, everyone takes notes, asks questions, and wants to meet me after the talk." It's the change in mindset that makes us learn better and faster in a more organized manner.

By developing and building relationships, which takes a lot of your valuable time, you make it obvious that you have a massive interest in what you do. When you are able to build a level of trust, conducting effective mentoring or coaching is possible. Your interest in investing in others and being a coach or mentor is essential to your personal growth, business, and life.

As you grow in your experience doing deals, your desire to teach others will grow also. Good investors never forget what it was like when they got started and wanted some guidance. They also realize what an impact they can make to new investors. Somewhere deep inside, they eventually feel a calling to help those newer wannabe investors.

Mentoring as a Sales Rep versus as a Sales Agent

Mentors may or may not choose a fee for their services. As a result, they can be placed in one of two categories: sales rep or sales agent. Sales representatives work to benefit the growth development and volume of the company they represent. On the other hand, a sales agent works for a commission based on sales.

If you mentor as a sales *rep*, you may opt to work for your clients, without pay, to help them grow and establish an independent business with long-term goals for gaining financial independence. If you decide to coach or mentor as a sales *agent,* you are explicitly working to be paid for your services. It is fine if you help others as an agent expecting a fee or commission for your professional time and guidance. If that is your livelihood and you can help them learn fast and complete great deals, then you are worth every penny you are paid for those services.

Sales reps are about closing deals. You close escrow and the deal is done. Being an agent is about representation. Both roles allow for the capacity to interact as coaches or mentors, guides or partners. Either chosen role is not about taking ownership but about helping to educate for growth, insuring due diligence, revealing disclosures, facilitating the deal, and mitigating risk.

You can still close deals yourself, but if you choose to coach or mentor others, you assume a lot more responsibility with a lot less money in the deal or from a closed transaction. I have found that when I am mentoring someone, making money is a secondary issue for me compared to supporting others' success. And, as my wife always says, "You're not making a sale—you're making a *fortune*!" She understands that there is no better way to grow your own fortune than by helping others find their fortunes first.

Personally, I have never charged a fee because I really find that the most rewarding work I can do is to provide my time, knowledge, and money to help others close deals. The prevailing philosophy is that if you are good at something, you have the right to charge a fee and get paid for your services. But if you're great, you have the privilege to give yourself away.

If you are not ready to be a mentor, but you wish to work with one, please ensure the following is determined in choosing your mentor:

- There should be no reluctance for answering your tough *questions*

- Dazzling presentations should not hide poor *responsiveness* and clear communication

- Have a clear understanding of *market value* as a variable in the deal

- Ensure the coach or mentor is a *full-time* investor—not a part-time consultant—in order to understand and explain the current market

- Avoid working with a *relative* or close friend, which may allow exposure of personal data you might not want family members to know about

- Have a definitive understanding of any *fees* involved between the coach and the student—the mentor and the mentee

- Control the direction of the deal instead of allowing the mentor to control your way of thinking

- Be sure to ask for references from other clients or partners and see how *googleable* they are

- Confirm active involvement in a previous deal so this is not something new to both parties

- Expect that others involved in the deal can speak highly of the mentor or coach—and yes, you should ask whether they have experience together

When you enter into this relationship between mentor and mentee, you must be sure it is working for both parties. If it isn't, you should find ways that will satisfy you both to avoid any misunderstandings, or you should terminate the relationship and move on.

Being a Guide to Those in Need

What made it so tough to get your first deal? What was holding you back from buying your first investment property? Five roadblocks that keep new investors from moving on are:

1. Not enough time

2. Not enough money

3. Not enough know-how

4. Not understanding how to acquire and use private and hard money

5. Not understanding the legal complications and contracts being used

These issues can also be a challenge when you assume the role of coach or mentor. If you haven't straightened these things out, you need to work on them before you decide to be a mentor yourself. Once you do enough deals—whether failing, winning, or breaking even—you will be ready to help others. Finally, if your mentor displays any of these poor characteristics, you need a different mentor. Overcoming these roadblocks is so important for both parties that I will address each of them.

1. **You don't have *enough time* to do real estate deals.** Someone once said, "*I don't have time* is the grownup version of *the dog ate my homework*." It's reflective of being lazy, not being dedicated enough, and always having excuses. Really? Who wants to work with someone like that? If you are time-management challenged, that's the first thing you need to fix or get a coach to help you with. Time is one of the three essential things you need to do a deal. Not having enough time is a complete myth. It's a phrase used to cover up your inadequacies when you face a challenge. You are only going to have enough time to do things that really matter, and if you don't have time to make real estate deals, either reprioritize things so you do, or quit right now and save yourself a lot of frustration.

2. **You don't have *enough money* to be involved directly in acquisitions and sales.** The secret to real estate investing has always been the same: "Don't wait to *buy* real estate. Buy real estate and *wait*." Because the economy and the markets constantly go up and down, historically, it's the wait that is always worth it. That said, it's still fair to ask: When is the right time to *buy*? The simple answer is when it fits your portfolio, completes an objective, and moves you toward reaching your goal. Usually, that means positive cash flow or other financial gain on a sale.

   One thing is certain: You must have money, in one form or another, to buy a property. The secret is that it doesn't have to be your own money. You can borrow from family, invest from your 401K or savings account, or insert hard money or private money. There are other options, such as selling stocks or other assets, but the essential thing to do is to put money to work that *will* grow more money for you. Two things to consider are: 1) you are making money every month on every transaction, and 2) you never invest in a property relying on it to grow in value; you can expect it to increase in value, but never be in a position where the deal requires it. That's called speculating or gambling, and it is an unneeded risk for any investor. You should opt for a long-term strategy based on realistic expectations, and you should spell out those expectations in your business strategy or plan.

3. **You don't have *enough know-how* to put together deals or see them through to closing.** If you don't have the knowledge, then you should be using a mentor. It takes knowledge to buy and sell homes. Your knowledge will grow with every new transaction you work, whether that is on your own or with a coach. The best ways to grow your real estate knowledge are to:

- Get a real estate license and work part-time or full-time.

- Network, network, network.

- Become a research expert on properties and their related demographics.

- Know the numbers required to complete the transaction.

- Learn from a mentor or coach.

4. **You don't know how to *acquire private or hard money* to make the deal work.** Getting money is always thought of as the hardest part of putting together a deal when, in fact, it's the easiest. But when you get started, it can feel like a black hole. Fear and pride are usually the culprits that hold you back. It's no shame to admit that you don't know how something works; if you're dedicated to doing this deal, you'll push your fear aside. Look back in Chapter 2 for how to find money or use new contacts you might learn about from your coach.

5. **You don't understand the *legal complications and contracts* required to close a deal.** You'll need to know many things in great detail, and most new investors are afraid those things may be too complicated. To overcome this issue, just remember it is like riding a bike. You will have a number of trials, but over time, you will learn something you never forget how to do. The most important things to know in this category are:

- Financial terms, processes, and major types of loans

- Seller assistance in closing the deal

- Purchase agreements and contracts

- Escrow processes and procedures

- Which parts of a contract are negotiable

- How to use amendment or changes

- Varieties in tenancy used for deeds and title

- How closing costs are determined

- Limits and uses of creative (non-conventional) financing

We could put all these challenges under the umbrella of due diligence. Never forget your due diligence methods when making a deal.

We all reach the point where we need "just-in-time" training—when we just need one question answered so we can make the next move. Nobody has ever known what to do by chance. There is always a learning curve. Having a mentor is a great way to make that curve easier to maneuver as you continue your real estate investment journey.

Summary

This chapter outlined how mentors can get involved with new investors and help guide them as they navigate through their initial real estate deals. It also taught the new investor what to expect from a mentor. In the next chapter, we'll discuss wealth building and present methods of accountability for both mentors and mentees.

Chapter 11

TEACHING OTHERS—*THE EDUCATION*

"A leader's job is not to do the work for others, it's to help others figure out how to do it themselves, to get things done, and to succeed beyond what they thought possible."

— Simon Sinek

Whether you are going to be a mentor or use a mentor, you must understand that the relationship's purpose is for the mentee to learn new information and strategies to improve his or her ability to make smart deals. I stress *learning* because it is so different from teaching.

In a previous career, I managed a very large training and development program that serviced multiple countries and provided daily training classes for hundreds of new trainees every week. My talent was in planning, directing, and controlling. I was not a great trainer or educator, so I made sure I surrounded myself with the best trainers to be found. Those trainers ensured that it was about *learning*—not about *training*. It's not about what you teach; it's about the transfer of knowledge and skills that changes students into performers.

Most educational systems are still producing people who are good at remembering what they read so they can pass an exam. However, we need to educate new investors so they can apply what they learn in live situations. Simply answering their questions so they will pay for your boot camp is not enough. Information is cheap—education is expensive—learning is priceless. Mentors provide *learning objectives* instead of *training objectives* because a significant difference exists between evaluating teaching versus evaluating learning. Does teaching change things—we're not sure how little or how much. Does an education change things—again, we're not sure. Many of the richest men and women in America have accrued their fortunes without completing a formal education at a large university. Does learning change things? Of this we can be sure: learning has the capacity to change things—if it is applied. Only when *learning* occurs have we reached the plateau of knowledge and skills gained where we know, and can accurately measure, that the individual has the capacity for expected gains.

All the things we discussed so far must be reviewed in your role as a mentor—from the concept of deal-making to development and application of the business plan. Be stubborn about your goals, but be flexible about your methods and objectives. There's more than one way to reach your goals, but if you can't measure them and you don't have a plan to accomplish your objectives, you probably will never actualize those goals.

Wealth-Building 101

As stated previously, the first thing to do if you want to build wealth is to own your own home. That may sound like a somewhat obvious way to get started, but it is also a very good way. Unfortunately, this little step is overlooked by a lot of people. Just take a look at how many people are still renting a property instead of buying one. Now, of course, the relationship between rent and housing prices varies from country to country and even from area to area. But wherever you go, you will still find people renting because they believe "I don't have enough money to buy a house." In reality, it would be much cheaper for them to buy!

When you rent, you are pretty much flushing your money down the toilet. Of course, you are getting the pleasure of living, but the point is you're not building anything long-term. Every dollar you spend on rent is a dollar you will never see again. Whereas if you own your own home, instead of paying rent, you will be paying your mortgage. Even though mortgages have a lot of variety these days, the basics are practically always the same. Every month, you make a payment, which consists of two parts: interest and principle. The interest part can be compared to rent. Those dollars are gone with the wind; you will never hear from them again. However, the part of the payment that goes to the principle is money you keep. Every dollar used to pay off the principal is a dollar you put in your own pocket.

So if you're thinking about family wealth-building and you don't own your own house yet, change that situation and get some experience. It's a great first step toward building your capital, and in many cases, it just makes more sense financially. It can also supply a range of opportunities for accelerating the process of building your net worth. When real estate prices go up, so does your property's value. Whereas the money you owe the bank—your mortgage—remains the same. In other words, owning your own home helps you build your net worth. Compare this situation to paying rent—your net worth does nothing. However, your landlord's net worth is doing very nicely in this scenario, and he or she will probably love you for it. So if you get a warm fuzzy feeling about making somebody else rich at your own expense... keep renting. If you would rather build your own capital instead... buy your own house! Many homeowners have accumulated more money through appreciation of their property than by working a full-time job for many years.

Now, before you go out and buy the first property you lay your eyes on, don't forget that some security measures are in order.

As you may know, real estate prices do not always go up, and they certainly don't go up in a straight line. Unbelievably, this fact can be shocking to some people, as well as an ugly reminder for those who overlooked it in the past.

If, for some reason, you have to sell your home in a down market, it can be a costly adventure. You wouldn't be the first to end up with a house worth considerably less than the mortgage resting on it. So make sure to keep some slack. In the long run, real estate prices have always been on the rise, but in any cycle, there are down periods. By keeping some slack and being patient, you will be able to sit through these times and profit from the long-term up-trend.

A major aspect of wealth-building is having the correct knowledge of how to pay taxes and use the tax laws to protect your investment. Taxation presupposes private ownership of wealth. If a government owned all the wealth in a society, including the wealth embodied in people, it would obtain all income, and there would be nothing to tax. No government has gone to such extremes in concentrating the wealth of a society in its own hands. Even in highly socialized societies, such as the former Soviet Union, people are permitted, subject to restrictions, to own household goods, savings accounts, and money. Taxation, therefore, becomes feasible. Nevertheless, the more wealth a government itself owns, the less that taxation is necessary because revenue from asset management is a substitute for tax receipts.

Whether you're investing only once or on a regular basis,

it's important to understand the differences between the main types of asset classes. Then you will know what to expect when you're investing so you can maintain control of your portfolio.

An asset class is a grouping or broad band of similar investments whose prices tend to move together. The concept of asset classes is important to understand because one common investment goal is to have a diversified portfolio—one made up of funds invested in different asset classes. This diversification can lower your overall exposure to risk since different asset classes will perform differently in different market conditions. It is important to know what type of asset classes you are currently invested in or intend to invest in to see whether your asset allocation (the amount invested in each asset class within your portfolio) is appropriate for your financial goals.

Whenever you choose a particular savings account or shares of stock, you are managing your asset allocation. Some things to consider when you select and stick with asset classes are:

- The type and amount of particular savings and investments you choose.

- Your *goals* and the money you will need to achieve them.

- Your investment *time* frame, which is usually set by how soon you intend to start taking money from your portfolio.

- How much *risk* you are willing to accept with the investment returns you need or want. Your risk tolerance will help determine your asset allocation. Your financial adviser can make sure you understand the risks associated with investing in each asset class.

Many low-income households are made up of retirees living on monthly payments from designated asset classes. Even if standard measures do not capture some of the income these households receive, the housing cost burden for these renters is substantial. But many employed renters are also in this group. Indeed, wages and salaries account for half the aggregate income reported for bottom-quintile households. Their earnings are usually insufficient to avoid paying more than 30 percent of income for housing.

Although housing cost burdens are much more common among lowest-income renters, affordability problems are moving up the income ladder. Between 2007 and 2009, 1.1 million more renters in the three middle-income quintiles faced at least moderate housing cost burdens. By 2009, more than one in five middle-income renters, and more than half of lower-middle-income renters, spent at least 30 percent of income on rent and utilities.

Improvements in affordability require both increasing renter incomes and moderating housing costs. But with persistently high unemployment, the prospects are dim for renter income gains, and a rising demand for rental housing may well put added pressure on rent costs. Moreover, global energy demand is almost certain to grow, further limiting the ability of the poorest renters to afford housing. As a result, the affordable housing shortfall is unlikely to improve any time soon. Innovations in housing production may, however, help bridge the gap between what low-income renters can afford and the rents necessary to supply and maintain affordable housing. In the meantime, most low-income renters will continue to face difficult tradeoffs between paying for housing and paying for other necessities.

We've already discussed how passive income is a primary channel for building wealth. It is an incredible tool that everyone should include in his or her retirement plan. With traditional investing, you have to rely on the stock market to increase your investment over time. If you have an active 401K or Roth IRA, then you understand that the longer you have your money invested, the more your money will grow. So if passive income from retirement accounts is a way you want to fund your retirement, you should start as early as possible and understand how to shift between aggressive mutual funds and more stable accounts such as bonds.

One of the most popular tactics for making money in real estate, due largely to numerous cable TV shows that promote it, is flipping houses. House flipping is the practice of buying a piece of real estate at a discounted price, improving it in some way, and then selling it for a financial gain. In reality, the flipping model is quite similar to the "buy low, sell high" model of most retail businesses. The most popular type of property to flip is the single family home. An experienced house flipper will buy a home for 70 percent of its current value minus any rehab costs. For example: Home A would be worth $100,000 if it were in good condition, but it needs $20,000 worth of work. A typical house flipper will purchase the home for $50,000 ($100,000 x 70 percent – $20,000) and seek to sell it for the full $100,000 when completed.

One of the key aspects of flipping a house is speed. A house flipper will attempt to buy, rehab, and sell the property as quickly as possible to ensure maximum profitability and to avoid many months of expensive carrying costs. These carrying costs include monthly bills such as financing charges, property taxes, condo fees (if applicable), utilities, and any other maintenance bills required to keep the house in good financial standing.

Flipping is not a "passive" activity; instead, it is just like an active day job. When an investor stops flipping, he stops making money until he starts flipping again. Many investors choose to use flipping to fund their day-to-day bills, as well as to provide financial support for other, more passive investments.

Rental properties are the more appropriate model for passive income because they produce cash flow every month. They keep producing cash flow as long as you own the property. The great part about passive income is the money comes in every month without you having to sell your investment or worry about running out of money when you retire. The returns are also better with rental properties because your cash flow is producing about a 20 percent cash-on-cash return, and that does not even include equity pay down on loans or appreciation. We look at appreciation on rental properties as a bonus while stock market investors actually depend on it. Another great thing about real estate passive income is that your rental income increases with inflation.

My model for real estate investing incorporates a hybrid of flipping and passive income. I use Lease with Option contracts. These can be one single contract or two separate contracts. One contract is the actual lease where the buyer is paying rent until the purchase is made. The other contract is the option contract.

I advertise to people who want to buy, but who can't get a mortgage due to a life situation that has occurred, such as bankruptcy, foreclosure, a loan to value issue, or a debt to income issue. My target buyer is someone who wants to buy a home but the banks have turned him down due to his financial situation. As the owner, I assume the risk that the banks will not. Since I almost always buy with cash, I can build terms to help the person buy. The option contract is similar to a First Right of Purchase.

In my Lease Options, I ask the buyer to pay a 3 percent option fee and pay the market value of rent for the property he will eventually own. I give the 3 percent fee back to him when he executes the option to buy. It is usually enough to help with the down payment. During the option period, we work together to fix his financial status so he can qualify for a regular loan. Usually, the person has a credit issue, and I am happy to pay for his credit repair as long as he does the things his credit counselor requires.

This type of contract keeps me from having to use a property manager. I also repair anything within the first ninety days, but after that, all costs for repair and maintenance are on the tenant. And the tenant will take very good care of the property since it is more than just a rental. It is a property he can call his home. It's a win-win for everyone involved. I get passive income for the time he is on the lease, and I get my flip money on execution of the sale.

You can make 100 percent profit or much more using lease options. Here is a very real example where I made a nice profit for a family who enjoy and love their home today:

- Cost of property I purchased $18,000
- Cost of rehab $12,000
  (needed considerable upgrades)
- Property sold for $68,500
- Rental income $32,400
  ($900 month for 36 months)
- Cost to carry $ 6,500
  (taxes, insurance, closing costs, etc.)

A total of $36,500 was needed to buy, fix, and hold this property. I made just over $100,000 back on the deal with almost $65,000 of that being pure profit. I received monthly income for three years, with no maintenance fees or property management, and made a tidy sum for reinvesting at the end of the deal.

If you are interested in wealth-building for your family—and you should be—you will have to develop a portfolio that meets your long-term goals using a variety of assets and income-producing methods.

The Education of a Real Estate Investor

When you begin as a real estate investor, you must understand that, like other complex activities, you will learn as you go. Everyone wants to be successful at it, but most people aren't. It isn't because they can't be; it's just that they don't know how, or they are hunting for the elusive shortcut to get rich quick. You cannot simply shortcut the accumulation of knowledge and skills that you need to succeed in this business. You must learn to earn.

If *anyone* could do it, there wouldn't be any room left for you to get in the game. You just cannot be totally prepared to make a deal on your own. If you have a part-time mentor, you will have access to an important support tool known as just-in-time training. That is, training on a specific area without spending a lengthy period of time on learning an entire process. It's really worth your time to invest in it. If you don't, I can assure you that you will get stuck somewhere in the process.

As with most skills, deal-making doesn't require you to be a genius. But it does take grit and determination. Longtime mathematician guru Ronald Nagrodski has stated this unmitigated fact: "I *can* is more important than IQ." Having a high Intelligence Quotient (IQ) has a lot to do with your DNA, intellect, and environment. Having an "I can" attitude is based on goal-directed behavior you can utilize for a chosen accomplishment.

Having said that, an accepted level of knowledge is required to understand the world of real estate investing if you desire to live and progress in that world. It requires an inexact amount of skills and knowledge, all dependent on what level of investments you are making and the relationships required to make those deals work.

Real estate education has traditionally focused on a series of discrete subject areas such as planning and valuation, supported by context-setting learning in economics, finance, and technology. The focus of assessment has frequently been on transactional activities, undertaking valuations, managing landlord and tenant problems, or being examined in economics, finance, and landlord and tenant law. In general, undergraduate real estate education has followed a similar syllabus for the past two decades, although teaching, learning, and assessment practices have evolved during this time.

With a couple of rare exceptions (lottery, inheritance, etc.), there are really only three main areas from which people can generate wealth and true financial independence for themselves:

- Successfully investing in the stock market

- Operating a successful business

- Successfully investing in real estate

But it's not nearly enough merely to select from the three and expect that results will occur according to a grand vision. Desired results can only come by creating a *successful* endeavor within any of these fields. And in each case, becoming thoroughly educated about the subject is the price that must be paid.

Warren Buffett, probably the most recognizable successful investor in businesses ever, has devoted his entire life to studying and evaluating companies to determine an accurate value of their stock so he can decide whether or not to invest in it or purchase it outright.

Certainly, operating a successful business requires the entrepreneur to become highly educated in his or her products in addition to the market, marketing, general business knowledge, cash flow, customer service, bookkeeping, accounting, sales, employee practices, systems, and more.

The same holds true for investing in real estate. For success to occur in real estate (and everything else), a person must commit fully and dedicate himself to be not just educated, but an expert. The first step needs to be a conscious decision to acquire whatever knowledge is necessary to succeed.

If real estate investing becomes your field of choice, commit to being an A+ student. A proper *education* is critical to your success. There's no shortage of information or direction. Bookstores and libraries have shelves filled with relevant resource material. The Internet serves as a virtually endless source of information as well as a gateway to various forms of training. Real estate investing clubs, associations, and networks are also plentiful.

Only about 1 percent of our population is considered wealthy, and only 3-4 percent become what could be classified as financially independent. This pattern has been repeated consistently for numerous generations, probably even centuries. I sus-pect the primary reason is because people tend to dabble. They don't take the time to comprehend the effort required to obtain the knowledge necessary for the level of success they desire. I also believe that if people would choose to become fully dedicated and take the actions necessary for success, many more would become members of the financially-free 5 percent.

Real estate investors account for much of the world's wealth, and real estate investing can be very rewarding when the price is paid. That price is the knowledge that comes from a proper education or mentorship.

Defining Methods of Accountability

I manage my business assets using a two-tiered structure I have labeled as Above the Line and Below the Line. When add-ed together, these two areas contain 100 percent of the actions required to optimize my business practices and procedures effec-tively and efficiently. Above the Line contains all the actions I personally must conduct, such as looking at the numbers before making decisions to buy or sell, balancing the accounts, writing checks, or signing closing documents. The actions Below the Line are things I contract out such as repairs, tax planning and report-ing, and home inspections. I put things below the line that make my time inefficient or require a licensed contractor or specialist. For example, my time is not being used efficiently by being present for evictions, doing my own home inspections, or conducting background and credit checks on potential buyers.

Even though I delegate, or contract out, some of my business activities, I still hold myself accountable for each action by reviewing and reporting everything accomplished. To be accountable is to report, explain, or justify, and then to be answerable and responsible. Having a sense of accountability reflects and demonstrates the ownership necessary to achieve desired results—to see it, own it, solve it, and do it.

Of course, such accountability requires a level of ownership that includes making, keeping, and answering to your business and personal commitments. This perspective embraces both current and future efforts. To create a culture of accountability is to define clear results within your business plan or strategy. Make sure you achieve results rather than just do the job.

The real value of accountability stems from the ability to influence events and outcomes before they happen. That influence helps to revitalize your business character, strengthen competitiveness, heighten innovation, improve the quality of your products and services, and increase the responsiveness of your private business to meet the objectives established to reach your goals.

To develop a sense of accountability, you have to have clear roles, team leadership, and individual ownership specifically defined in your business plan or strategy. I define all responsibilities in my business plan by using the Above the Line and Below the Line concept. When roles and processes are ambiguous, people struggle to be accountable. Remove as much confusion as possible about who is doing what and how each person will proceed. Also, develop a sense of ownership for team results; a sense of ownership is achieved by focusing on processes and establishing an obligation for all involved to seek information as well as receive feedback.

Accountability is the obligation of a person to keep records of properties, documents, or funds. These records show identification data, gains, losses, dues-in, dues-out, and balances on hand or in use. If you are not balancing your portfolio and each of those assets at least monthly, you are putting your money at grave risk. My commitment to accountability is the simple action of briefing the status of assets and existing contracts monthly to my business partner—which fortunately for me—is my wife.

Summary

The last two chapters were about roles played by mentors and mentees and the expectations they should have for one another. Now we will take a more objective approach by defining a results-oriented concept for maintaining enthusiasm, growing the business, and providing direction and feedback.

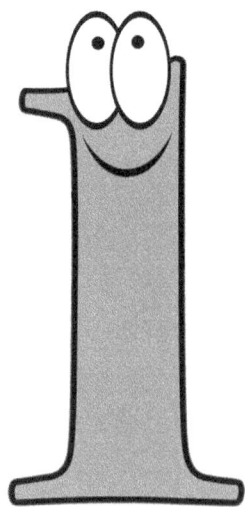

Chapter 12

MENTORING FOR RESULTS—*THE APPLICATION*

*"A mentor is someone who allows you
to see the hope inside yourself."*

— Oprah Winfrey

New members will always be joining the wide, wide, world of real estate investing. These new investors must be careful and deliberate in their choices. They need to minimize risk, and the only way they can avoid the land mines and find the gold mines is by having a mentor as their guide. As a mentor, it is your responsibility to issue advice, challenges, and feedback. Everyone is open to good advice, many are not so good at challenges, and very few are actually open to criticism. Criticism seems to bring a fear factor to success, but its intention is to help you grow. It can be embraced as a way to correct some of the things you do in order for you to get better results. It's amazing how everyone wants to get better but won't accept criticism as the conduit to progress. In the words of Steve Ross, the former CEO of Time Warner, "The only way to avoid criticism is to do nothing." A mentor and his or her learner should understand this principle upfront so it will not be a roadblock to success when it happens. And it is *supposed to happen* if a new investor wants to grow.

The most important part of mentoring is to be objective, maintain enthusiasm, and educate new real estate investors in the right direction. Excellent mentors don't have a big head, but they do have a big heart and are compassionate and patient. If you go without a mentor, you're on your own. You may get lucky without one, but you'll be a whole lot luckier with one.

Maintaining a High State of Objectivity

Setting objectives and goals is an essential activity because it allows you and your partners to recognize and adopt your business' vision and mission. Clearly identified goals enable the transformation of a vision into actionable tasks. We discussed this in Chapter 5, but it is worth revisiting as we discuss the importance of objectivity. Measuring our actions is important; think of it as a report card on our growth toward success. Those measurements are something we must pay close attention to because if we are not moving toward success, we are probably failing. Whatever time you must sacrifice to educate yourself and heed the advice of your coach or mentor will be the best time you spend growing. To paraphrase motivational speaker Zig Ziglar, "You don't have to pay the price for success, but you must pay the price for failure."

One giant step will get you there, but it consists of a series of small steps up the staircase to your destination. Each of those small steps is measurable and requires that you monitor them to identify areas of weakness and strength and make any required adjustments. It is recommended that you also evaluate the success of your achievements and results with your mentor or coach. He or she will be completely focused on the results and where you end up after completion of a task, action, or objective. Your mentor is dedicated to providing advice, not dictating it. You won't grow if you are a puppet just doing as you're told.

When you maintain a high state of objectivity, you are protecting yourself from the traps of biases, prejudices, guesswork, and false expectations. More or less, you are observing specific measured results uninfluenced by emotions or personal prejudices. You are making yourself take action to balance the books, read each document, focus on the outcomes, and react to facts, not feelings. When you stay objective, you are lighting the path toward revealing the outcomes of a provable scientific result.

Most of the information you gather in today's world of real

estate investing comes from biased, non-objective information that seemed to work years ago but doesn't work today and is not proven by truly objective matter. If you, like me, ever purchased a boot camp or "system" from a seminar guru, you likely bought it based on the emotional and motivational feeling you had at the moment. More likely than not, you were misled—not by the speaker but by your own lack of objectivity. You had the same thought most people have at a casino: "Why not me? Let's gamble my money and see whether I can be a winner!" When my wife and I go to casinos—and we go a lot—we know we can win every day and every night. Objectively, all we have to do is walk away when we're ahead. But the thrill of the game can be addicting when you are in the middle of the room and there is so much going on. Passion and excitement take over because, in reality, we're not there to win a few hundred bucks—we are there to win a hundred thousand bucks. We are there to win the big jackpot, the million dollars at the progressive payout slots. Objectivity couldn't be further from us when we act on our emotions.

It should be just plain common sense that you can't run a business that way—but many have tried. When you're playing with your family's wealth, you must maintain a high state of objectivity. Work with your mentor or coach to learn more about being objective in all your business activities, and learn how to measure your results to gauge how you are doing in achieving your goals.

Generating and Maintaining Enthusiasm

We know from current studies—and it probably does not

surprise you—that less than 50 percent of American employees are happy with their jobs. According to a New York-based economic research group, the last time more than 50 percent were happy was in 2005. The irony here is that when the same people were asked whether they plan to stay with their current employers, 56 percent said, "Yes" and another 33 percent said, "Possibly."

You can see for yourself what is wrong with this picture. It is almost always the best employees who want to move on. And that may leave the more under-committed employees with the company. I don't mean this in a disrespectful way, but those who just need a paycheck and benefits will put up with bad bosses and unhappiness in the workplace. And understandably, employees often have no choice but to hang on to jobs they need to support their families. But that doesn't make them happy employees or overly productive in an austere or unappreciative environment. A lack of employee commitment returns to employers an abundance of inefficiency, low productivity, weak customer service, and high absenteeism.

When you make the move to self-employed real estate investor, you are leaving that world behind. Having explained all that, you assume the sole responsibility to keep yourself motivated and enthusiastic about your new endeavor. I remember how excited I felt when I made my second million in real estate; for the first time, I really understood my sense of identity and accomplishment. When I had a corporate job, I would wake up in the morning and, while taking a shower, think to myself, "Oh, buggers, I have to go to work today!" But when I became a full-time investor, I got much less sleep, and when I took a shower in the morning, all I could think was, "Oh, yeah, I can't wait to get to work this morning!"

When you are self-employed, you don't think about regular hours because you are consumed with growing your business 24/7. You are working for your own signature business and spotlighting to the world your brand, responsiveness, and capability. That is when you begin to push yourself to new dimensions you never knew existed—and then some.

The important takeaway here is that being a real estate investor—having your own business—is highly motivational and extremely involving. So involve yourself with actionable things to keep your motivation high at all times about day-to-day operations. Again, having a mentor or coach will help you complete achievable challenges that continue to stimulate your high motivation and zeal for business.

Here are some tips for actionable things you can do to stay motivated:

- **Read a real estate book at least once a month.** At first you may think you don't have time, but you will quickly discover that you have an awful lot of dead time, such as waiting in the dentist office, having lunch alone once in a while, or traveling on a plane.

- **Volunteer to help other investors.** It is by giving that we receive so much and remain so aware of, and inspired by, the world around us.

- **Stay away from negative environments, negative movies and TV shows, and negative people.** Banish them all to the fifth dimension—out of your life. Learn that it is okay to "unfriend" others who generate negative campaigns on social media.

- **Attend free real estate seminars and cash-flow games in your area.** Hanging around positive like-minded investors is very motivational.

- **Develop a mindset of complimenting others.** It could be, "Wow, I love the color of your hair," or "Where did you find that nice shirt? I was looking for a similar one online," or "Those earrings are absolutely gorgeous. Where did you find them?" Don't worry; as soon as you start practicing, you'll find an endless string of nice compliments to give.

- **Look through magazines—but only focus on the advertisements.** You can do that at a bookstore, a drugstore, or at a beauty salon. You'll get fresh ideas when you do this, so make sure you have a pen with you.

- **Count your blessings once a week.** You can just think about it, or you can actually add to your personal journal all the positive things that happened during your week. If you are running out of positive things that happened that week, go back and review this list from the top.

Stretching and Growing—Expanding the Business

You must constantly expand your business acumen by seeking a continuing depth of knowledge about your market, products, services, and profits. Growing your business means growing in knowledge, spending more time in it, and resourcing more avenues of money to make the deals happen. Never lose focus of growing your real estate investment business in these three areas: knowledge, time, and money.

Expanding your business will depend on your knowledge of the market and your profit growth. Your growth may lead to a need for larger markets or more niche markets. It all depends on what is working for you and what is not. Expansion may lead you to developing collaborative profit-sharing with property managers, rehabbers, or other investors. Your mentor or coach can help you with forecasting concepts to analyze possibilities or new investments.

Every business expands, starting with day one of business. As deals are analyzed and offered, opportunities expand and your contact list grows. As you progress, you and your coach will analyze the numbers to determine your break-even point. Breaking even is simple double-entry accounting, no different from balancing your checkbook, where your income matches your expenses. Pushing past your break-even point, you become more aware of possibilities for expanding your business.

As your business continues to expand, you still must analyze your numbers because you may reach the point where you can't manage all of the tasks, meetings, and responses needed. That is the tipping point where you need to expand your business.

It's the point we all want to reach, but it requires decisions on possibly adding other people to your team or subcontracting out (below the line) work.

Break-even analysis is a simple mechanism used to determine when your investment business will be able to cover all its expenditures and begin to make a profit. For a startup business, it is crucial to know your costs for startup; those costs present you with the knowledge you need to generate enough sales revenue to pay the ongoing expenses related to running your business. Before embarking on expansion, be sure there is consistent bottom-line profit and that the company has experienced steady growth over an extended period, which could be six months or more. Please be sure to work with your coach, mentor, or tax planner to develop strategies and objectives to increase profits before you ever consider expansion.

Before you can ever think about expanding your business, serious market research must be done. Collecting market research data and statistics will help you meet the needs of active and potential customers and contribute to your gaining a better understanding of the business. Information can be extracted from online searches, trade publications, government bodies, industry associations, customers, and market reports that assist in reviewing business and marketing plans.

Once you have a clearer insight of market trends, implementing practices that achieve business growth will not be difficult. Then it is important for the revised marketing strategy to reflect the research and for the practices to be implemented properly.

Frequent revising is crucial to any business' ongoing

growth. As the company expands, revise and update the business plans regularly. Accommodating a change in direction for the business also requires regular updating of a business plan. As your market expands, you will need to reconsider issues like risk management, marketing, insurance, intellectual property, finances, and your business' structure. An open marketing plan provides direction and ensures a systematic, precise approach to promoting and expanding a business. Increasing efforts in marketing and promotion can be a crucial step toward developing and improving your business and also increasing your customer base. If any notable changes are made to a business, the advertising materials must also be updated, for example, business cards, logos, and signage. If a need exists for overseas business expansion, again good market research is required to examine the target market.

Providing Feedback and Direction

I strongly recommend you have a coach or mentor as you grow to learn the real estate investing business. If you choose not to do that, you will probably lose money or be suckered into bad deals and end up gravely discouraged. Ask me how I know that! Matter of fact, ask your coach how she knows it. It happens to all of us who try to go it alone. We all have testimonials that end up with the same recourse, "I wish I had know about that before I got into the deal."

Having a mentor is a special relationship of partnering. It's a partnership because both sides have responsibilities to commit to one another. If either one of you is not responsible, then the partnership will fail. Normally, as a mentor myself, the only thing I expect is an enjoyable positive relationship in which I sense I am doing something worthwhile by helping someone else achieve his or her goals. When I sense the relationship is not working, then I lose my motivation.

The best way to establish a partnership with your mentor is for you to explain your clearly-defined objectives, the problems you may be facing, and how you expect your mentor to help you. Then, of course, show appreciation and respect for his or her time. The most challenging aspects of the mentor-mentee relationship are feedback and direction. It is best for both parties to articulate their expectations for feedback and direction within the first two meetings.

There are two types of appropriate feedback:

- **Positive Feedback:** Positive feedback applies when the mentee has done exceptionally well in an assignment or in any aspect of his business. The purpose of positive feedback is to make the mentee aware of how well he performed, how his performance is linked to expected behaviors, how he achieved his measurable objectives, and to reinforce good performance.

- **Constructive Feedback:** Constructive feedback is applicable when the person has not behaved in line with expectations. Its purpose is to highlight where and why the performance was not up to expectations and explore how the mentee can do better next time. Again, even constructive feedback is used as a positive way to improve future performance.

An essential element in implementing effective feedback is creating an atmosphere of mutual regard and trust. When a feeling of trust has been built, it is easier for both partners in the mentoring relationship to give and receive feedback. Trust is like a mirror—once it's broken, you can never fully see yourself in it again. Or, as someone once said, "Never trust someone who lies to you, and never lie to someone who trusts you."

Make sure the mentee knows you are working toward a mutual objective—the mentee's success. Giving and receiving feedback can be a very positive experience for the mentee and the mentor as long as you both know that you share the same responsibility to promote the mentee's career.

When you give constructive feedback, it is necessary to acknowledge the mentee's successes and achievements in areas where he or she needs improving. You should always be precise in providing feedback. It is not helpful to say, "Your work is poor." It is much more useful to define the particular element of work that concerns you. Just like how we defined measures used in developing business objectives, feedback should identify the quantifiable elements that could be improved.

Feedback should be straightforward and simple. When deciding to give feedback as a mentor, plan on a small number of areas you want to cover. You don't wish to create a list of faults that could confuse and discourage the mentee. Offer to work with your mentee to develop solutions to any challenge he or she is encountering.

If you are on the mentor side of this partnership, please remember that your mentee probably does not have much experience with this type of feedback and direction. I have always found feedback easy to deliver if I precede it with a comment, such as: "Leonard, I have some constructive feedback to discuss with you concerning your time-management skills. Are you ready to go over this?" The simple act of introducing the way ahead gives the mentee a moment of preparation, and it gives you, the mentor, an opportune insight into his or her body language before you begin.

Providing and receiving feedback properly are both developmental skills that will enhance the partnership. Be sure to accept your responsibility in that. Feedback, however, sometimes requires a flow of discussion that either emits a challenge or provides recognizable advice on the direction you might want to consider.

You don't and can't get rich by just going to Starbucks for coffee. You can get rich when you create a product and provide a direction for others to be rich. Mentors and coaches help to co-construct or reconstruct a sense of direction for a lesser-experienced investor so they can thrive. Newer investors need to understand what it means to receive direction in order to become more effective in their business. This is much different from training, evaluating, or providing feedback. When you are providing feedback and you focus on objectivity, you are suggesting some options for the mentee to figure things out. Giving direction means *tasking* someone to accomplish a specific objective.

It is preferred that a mentor provide guidance instead of direction, but often an investor just does not have the experience to figure out the next move. A lot is involved in the process of directing. The goal-directed rule is that a mentor can steer someone in the right direction, but he or she should not force a change of direction. Every new investor should find a mentor to work with.

Now that you have the basic tools to begin real estate investing and you have a mentor to guide you, it's time to turn to how you can maintain your motivation and the enthusiasm you began with. In the next section, we'll look at the three most important things you can do to stay motivated: network, do volunteer work, and involve yourself in confidence-building activities.

Summary

The last four chapters, Section III of the book, were about preparing the mentor and mentee by explaining the roles they should play and their expectations of one another in working together on deals. The next few chapters, Section IV, are designed to help both mentors and mentees remain motivated in the pursuit of their work efforts. Networking and volunteering are important activities to keep you, the real estate investor, involved in the community and ensure you are recognized as a giver and someone people want to work with.

SECTION IV

STAYING MOTIVATED

"Success isn't a result of spontaneous combustion.
You must set yourself on fire!"

— Arnold H. Glasow

Motivation is the key to accelerating high performance and the pursuit of continuous improvement. Having said that, one of the most important lessons I learned in an executive capacity is that it is *not* necessary to attempt to motivate people. "Why not?" you may ask. All schools of management teach us about motivating employees. All our bosses tell us to keep our employees motivated. The practice and preachings are systemic and core to our management training.

In my experience, the reason you don't have to motivate your workers is because *they are already motivated*. You must find out, during interviews, what it is that motivates them and put them in a position where they can enjoy working in that capacity. Use their motivation to enhance performance that improves the effectiveness and efficiency of your operations.

The hit TV series *Undercover Boss* consistently shows motivated employees who, once recognized by their boss, experience a life-changing moment—a realization that someone really cares and wants to help them pursue the things that already motivate them. Somehow, it is hard for me to detach motivation from dreams. When people are motivated, they will find a way—they will create a way. What they will not create is an excuse.

There are only three chapters in this section, and they deal with three significant areas that can keep you motivated: Networking, volunteering, and constant self-improvement. They all work. They add to your very soul. They bring you closer to other positive people and help you remember how important we all are to each other.

Chapter 13

NETWORKING

"If you want to go fast, go alone.
If you want to go far, go with others"
— African Proverb

Networking is part science, part art, and dare I say, part psychology. People require an understanding of its mechanics, an individualistic way of conducting it, and means of applying it through second-tier contacts to reach their goals. The primary reason we network is to make contacts so we can develop relationships that build trust. While I never ask to help contacts buy or sell homes, I am sincerely interested in *their* contacts—their spheres of influence.

My primary method for efficient networking is to help with referrals. I've always found that giving referrals first is the best way to get referrals. Likewise, I can prove that helping others get business first is the best way to get additional business for myself. To use networking efficiently, and not waste your time at the wrong events, you need to know how to work a crowd, build trust, and attend a variety of events that better posture you for more business.

Working a Crowd

Networking builds the conduits by which information highways are built. If we go networking with the intention of "getting something," there is very little chance of success. If, however, we network to bring business to others, we will always succeed.

When we network, we build relationships that develop trust. We will meet some folks whom we immediately feel strong ties to, and then there are others whom we may not feel as strongly bound to. Do not treat those weaker relationships as any less powerful than the stronger ones you build. As Adam Grant, author of *Give and Take*, stated, "Strong ties provide bonds, but weak ties serve as bridges." Those we feel closer to usually travel in similar circles as we do, whereas the weaker relationships actually filter out to the masses by way of silent referral. And anyone who has been in sales a long time will agree that referrals are the most important part of building our business. Those weaker relationships have greater capacity to build our networks by allowing us to break into areas and groups we have never been in before.

I've been to many networking events where introductions are routinely done near the beginning of the meeting. Yet at most of these events, despite the awesome opportunity to make a big impression and become memorable to the group, most professionals go through a weak, unimpressive litany of what they do...and they end up sounding like every other professional in their industry (and most in the room), thereby failing to make a memorable impression.

Contrast this with the event promoter who has such a catchy jingle when he stands up to give his elevator speech that everyone in the room recites it with him! Or the children's party clown who blew a funny whistle before introducing himself, then stood up with a red nose on his face. Or the car wash/car detailing company owner who stood up and blew bubbles in the air as he introduced himself...and then gave a bottle of bubbles containing his company name and contact information to everyone in the crowd. Or the business adviser who gave out casino-style chips with the words, "Don't gamble with your business" printed on one side and his contact information on the other.

Compare the humdrum words of those who merely state their name, occupation, and company name (as if stating name, rank, and serial number) to the lawyer who stood up and said, "If you're working with a lawyer (or trying to work with a lawyer) who isn't calling you back, call me. I'll call you back!" BAM! In one sentence, he let everyone in the room know he knew one of the biggest customer problems in his industry—and he let everyone know he had a solution for it. I contacted him myself (because I was experiencing this problem at that very time!). Later, I referred another client to him, who eventually put him on retainer with his company...simply because he let me know at our very first meeting that he could solve one of the biggest problems with lawyers!

Compare this, as well, to the people who toss unfamiliar jargon around in their introductions, leaving the rest of us scratching our heads trying to figure out what they actually do!

Many of us spend an awful lot of time driving to, attending, and driving back from networking events because relationships are the name of the game in this competitive climate. What are you doing to differentiate yourself right from your introduction, let your customers know you understand their problems, show them you *are* the solution to those problems—and get them to notice and remember you?

Let's look at some important concepts for when you are networking and trying to make an impression, so you can ensure that our time and effort are not wasted.

If I don't know what you do, I can't use or recommend your services. Don't toss around jargon, abbreviations, or terms that people outside your industry won't recognize or understand. Never assume that everyone has the same knowledge you do. If you must use an acronym or industry term, be sure to explain it by saying,

"In other words..." or "which is just a fancy way of saying..." (remember that using humor *always* helps!) Explaining terms never hurts, but not explaining them will practically ensure that someone will not know them and will not ask for an explanation from fear of looking foolish.

If I don't know what to listen for after the meeting, nothing will trigger my memory so I can recommend you. Don't simply tell people what you do; tell them what situations occur out in the real world with which you can help. For example, the financial adviser who started out telling us he "worked with businesspeople and entrepreneurs to help them with their financial needs" wasn't helping me recommend his services until he came to a meeting one day and said, "If you know of people who have just had a change in their life circumstances, such as having a baby, getting married or divorced, or retiring, they can use my services." BAM again! Hearing the words and situations I could listen for out in the real world helped trigger my memory that my neighbor had just had a baby...and I could then make the recommendation. What life circumstances, conversations, and words can you have others listen for outside of the networking meeting that would trigger their memory of you and what you can provide, so they can recommend you?

If you don't make a memorable impression, I will forget I saw you at the meeting. Most business is not closed right at networking meetings—it's closed after them, by people who connect, begin, and nurture a relationship and create trust with each other. Remember: one meeting does not a relationship make. However, you can't even begin a relationship if you don't get someone to notice you and become interested in you in the first place.

Follow up with people after the meeting is over. Once you do begin a relationship, nurture it—don't stick people's business cards in a drawer and forget about them. However, don't assume you can send automatic emails, such as newsletters, either. Always get permission to send automated items and to make personal contact occasionally through handwritten notes, cards, clippings, and phone calls.

When you do follow up (or even when you first meet someone), seek to serve rather than to receive. Ask people what you might be able to do to help them, connect them with a resource you may have, or give advice without expecting anything in return. Remember what leadership expert John Maxwell says: "People don't care how much you know until they know how much you care." The principle of giving back is wonderful; the principle of giving before is better. When you show others you're willing to give, they respond in kind and give back to you.

The whole purpose of taking the time to network with others is to establish relationships, begin communications, and build trust and rapport...all of which helps others as well as helping you build your business over time.

Networking events are not sales efforts per se because they don't always (or even usually) produce immediate results. Effective, high-impact sales efforts are still needed to continue to build "NOW" business.

Referring First—to Get Referrals

The first step to getting referrals is not to ask for them. Getting is always about *giving first*, and nowhere could that be more true than in the business of getting referrals. From the moment of introduction, you should try to get your new contact to tell you all about what she does, determine whether you have mutual contacts, and then follow up to ask what is the best way you can send referrals her way. You may even ask whether the person can give you one or two sentences to put into a referral email. I keep a list of those referral statements in OneNote on my desktop so I can easily copy and paste them when I am chatting online with someone asking for a referral.

It is true that there is no better compliment to your business than receiving referrals from others. I actively give out a dozen or so referrals every week. As this has become part of my lifestyle, I have also noticed that I have at least fifty soft opportunities to give out referrals each week, but I only give out about twenty. So why don't I take advantage of every opportunity when I'm not sure about giving out a specific referral? On one hand, if I give out a referral and the person I refer doesn't do a good job, it's my own character that gets a dent in it. On the other hand, the situation might be in an area I know little about so I feel uncomfortable making that referral or recommendation. In some of those cases, I still say, "I know *of* someone who is in that business, but I've never actually used him myself."

You should actively be seeking out new sources at networking events to make referrals for. You need to do this a lot. You don't need to practice it as much as you should seek to become *polished* at what you do. As you practice more and more, you want to become a lean, mean referral machine—someone who is a natural—someone who *shines* at what you do.

However, receiving referrals is great only when you do it the right way—by helping others to get referrals first. Once you are acknowledged and recognized for your referral, other things will fall into place. Because you referred others to someone—your lawyer, dentist, plumber, hairdresser, etc., those people will take notice and then start referring potential real estate clients to you. Therefore, mastering the art of referral generation should begin with your own referral. Once people can like you, trust you, and think of you, your referrals will get in line.

Many real estate investors actually get paid well for a referral fee. That's a pretty attractive way for your contacts to be a little more motivated to get you a referral. Income earned from giving referrals is called wholesaling. That is where a third party (wholesaler) gets paid a referral fee (or finder's fee) for helping a seller find a buyer for the sale of his property. Some wholesalers actually get a fee from both sides of the transaction. Sometimes, they use an *assignment of contract*[1] and just sell the rights to the contract to another investor. They can make some pretty good money putting contracts together while not having to do very much work at all.

---

[1] An assignment of contract is where one party (usually as a buyer) enters into a contract with another (usually a seller) and reassigns a third party as the buyer. The purpose is to make money by selling interest in the deal but not going through the process of buying and then selling.

It is common practice for a real estate investor or real estate agent to refer a client, either a buyer or a seller, to a colleague when the transaction is based in a different state or market or requires specialized expertise. When the transaction closes, the investor pays a referral fee to the person who set up the contract. The referral fee, which is agreed to in advance, is usually a percentage of one transaction side or it can be a flat rate. The percentage of referral fees for residential real estate is usually much higher than for commercial because the work, knowledge, commission splits within the team, and expenses for commercial transactions are more extensive.

There are a lot of ways in your daily life to make and receive referrals. You can make good money with referrals, but you'll find the best and most continuing source of referrals is made with the long-term in mind. Please think about these ideas:

- Attend recurring networking events and provide continuing referrals.

- Use LinkedIn referrals; it's easier than most people understand.

- Provide a template and written paragraph about yourself when you meet.

- Take action on feedback from others; call or text right away.

- Be referable; make sure others understand what makes you unique.

- Create a list of referrals you are looking for and hand it out.

- Create ways for others to refer you by phone, website, or direct texting.

- Keep the pipeline going and add to both sides every day.

- Put a referral form on your website in case someone wants to contact you.

- Reward and thank your referring partners for all the referrals you get.

- Add to your daily email that you are looking for specific referrals.

- Always say thank you the next time you meet someone who referred you.

- Constantly ask for referrals using all forms of social media.

- Set a weekly goal of giving at least ten referrals to others.

You can do plenty of things to give and receive referrals each week. Beg if you have to. It may sound corny, but at least once in a while when I am at a networking event, I actually get down on my knees when doing introductions and ask for referrals. Doing so is always humorous, well-accepted, and has positive results. I've got to do what I've got to do, right?

Always remember that a *referral* is a recommendation. It's a high-quality lead and a high-probability prospect that is introduced to you or given by you. Don't forget, however, that each time a referral is used, the person who made the referral has his or her reputation on the line. If you refer a rehab worker to another investor and he does a rotten job, then you won't be getting any referrals in return. The person won't forget it. Be positive about giving referrals to others, but don't be too free to hand out names you don't really know very well.

Building Trust

Trust is a general and vital matter in whatever form of business you are dealing with. You get recommendations when people can trust you for what you are and what you do. In addition, trust takes you places you may not have imagined reaching anytime soon. It has the powerful effect of boosting your sales and making you feel confident about doing more.

The real estate business, from investors and rehabbers to agents and brokers, is an extremely competitive area, so it's very easy to create hard feelings. It's also easy to speculate with negative feelings when things don't go your way or people don't return calls or emails. Sometimes we view things as dishonest, condescending, unprofessional, and even personal. Please understand that this is a business, which requires a tough skin and a short memory. We tend to blame others a lot in this business, and a major reason why is because we all have a tendency to hold important information without sharing it and doing things to keep advantages on our side. If you're competing with other investors, that's just going to happen, but stay away from doing things that are dishonest and unethical because they will damage your character for a long time.

So many people are involved with this business who are not the competition, so we must maintain a high level of respect and trust to continue business with them. Some of the things you can do to build trust are to share, compliment others, avoid criticizing, keep your promises, and show appreciation for what others do.

You can build long-term positive relationships by sending simple short emails or phone calls to stay in contact with people. Effective communication is the key to maintaining bonding in a relationship; it goes far deeper than mere superficial association. If you are looking for such a connection with your clients, contractors, and other investors, then your efforts can go beyond just the formal routine of emails to establish a more personal human bond.

Do you know that personal notes are a great way to develop an affinity with clients? They introduce an emotional dimension to the communication that makes people feel appreciated and recognized. As an entrepreneur, when you acknowledge your customers as your greatest assets by devoting some time to writing a note to them, you actually make them feel special. In the corporate jungle, people start feeling that firms are out to hunt them down, and those firms are not concerned about anything other than their profitability. The selfless act of writing a personal note will set you apart from most firms while earning you a great reputation.

If you are wondering when and why you should send out these little personalized pieces, here are the answers: The notes can be written for a variety of messages you want to convey; for example, gratitude for staying with the firm during tough times, appreciating someone's feedback, sending wishes on an anniversary, thanking someone for a referral, or even apologizing for a slight inconvenience—all these reasons will make the recipient feel special, and in the long run, earn you loyal customers.

All you have to do is to review your email contacts and write a note once in a while to stay in contact with them and let them know you are thinking about them. While preparing your list, selection may be made based on the size or frequency of transactions someone has done with the company. However, a lot will also depend on the business strategy of the firm to decide on the criteria for selection. Each day, handwritten personal notes for a small number of clients can be prepared and sent so that the list is covered in a definite timeframe.

It's important to build trust—but guess what—you don't have to rebuild something that was never broken. Keep your character solid, be easy to work with, and don't talk badly about others.

We network to build relationships. We build relationships to develop trust. When we are at the level of trust, then we can work together.

An-Eventing We Will Go, an-Eventing We Will Go

Just like the old nursery rhyme, "a-hunting we will go," we want to play the events in town to get our brand out and let others know we are bona fide real estate investors, coaches, and/or mentors who can help others achieve their investment goals. To me, it's interesting to see all the different booths at an expo. Everyone has his or her own way of marketing a product. But let's face it; most of these companies sell the exact same product with a small spin on it. So is it possible to stand out amid all these competitors? What will give you the competitive advantage?

The answer is your booth—more specifically, how the people in your booth are explaining your products. Simply put—if the people working your booth aren't excited about the products they are selling, then neither will the buyers be. Are your booth people actively earning, using, showing off, and playing with your merchandise? If not, they need to be! Hundreds of potential customers are walking by, and if you're sitting in the dark corner of your booth, it's just not going to work.

How do promotion items factor into your booth's success? They make you memorable after the expo is over—provided they are creative. For example, think of something that can replace your generic business card. That idea alone will give you many ideas. Don't let your business cards end up in the wastebasket. (Note: That will never happen if your employees are passionate about what they are showing off.)

Make sure that even if your booth is small, it appears spacious. Be organized. Know, before you set foot on the show floor, exactly how you are going to approach your possible clients. When it comes right down to it, you can have all of the things I have mentioned, but you also need to have a great product or service. Having a great product takes passion, the same passion that needs to be transferred into your booth people.

Tips for Genuine Connecting

Networking is about working a crowd, giving and getting referrals, building trust, and attending a variety of events. In today's world, networking has more to do with connecting and genuinely caring about people than adding them to your address book until they can do something for you. The real question then is: How do you connect with people? Simply put, you just need to find a common ground upon which to build your connection. Here are a few ideas:

- **Develop a genuine interest in people.** Some of the most interesting and fascinating people are those who might not usually catch your networking eye. For example, that guy in the polo shirt and jeans when everyone else is wearing a blazer and slacks—come on! Surely anyone who does not know how to dress properly is not worth knowing. Pssst! That guy might be so sure of himself that he won't be bothered by convention, and he might just be the one you need to collaborate with on your next big project.

- **Really connect with people.** I always smile when I hear or even find it necessary to use the popular term B2B (Business to Business). Don't look now, but business is done P2P (Person to Person). Have you ever seen two businesses make a deal? No, but you've seen their owners or some other *person* making those deals.

- **Get past the titles and CVs and really find out who people are at a deeper level.** You might discover that their purpose resonates with yours and that you can work together to create or further something beneficial to both of you and others. Before you know it, you're making real deals and actual money, and that's so much more rewarding.

- **Check your image.** You can smell them from way across the room (I can anyway!)—those people at an event whose body language says, "I really don't belong here. If I had the guts to say, 'No' to my very ill mother, I'd be on the golf course with my crowd. *But* since I'm here, I might as well give out a few business cards." Building relationships and connecting require warmth, openness, empathy, friendliness, and being easy to approach. Be genuinely interested in the people you meet and listen to their stories. Being stiff, aloof, and only concerned about handing out your business card will not cut it in connecting. Remember, you're building relationships for the longterm.

- **Develop the necessary skills.** No, I am not suggesting that all you have to do to connect with people is to go where they are. Connecting effectively requires you to develop some key people skills and these three top the list. Listening allows people to tell you their stories and allows you to show you're genuinely interested in them. Small talk or the ability to talk to anyone about anything is critical to the process. Self-confidence is invaluable for enabling you to approach people and start conversations. After all, connecting is about building relationships.

- **Learn to give.** If it doesn't come naturally, you should really learn how to give. I don't mean the big $500 corporate gift. I mean the willingness to share an idea to help a person improve something, the free reports on your website, or the information-packed one-hour strategy session. Giving excites me big time. First of all, it's just the thing to do. Secondly, what you give truly comes back to you ten-fold. Don't worry about the "how"—it just does. Giving also builds trust, and people like to do business with people they trust. One of my colleagues has connected me to so many people, and some of those connections have been truly profitable. What a gift!

- **Learn professional etiquette.** Please! Many of your connections will come through attending events, so learn how to conduct yourself on these occasions. People remember people who are gracious, polished, and treat them with dignity. Furthermore, if you know how to handle yourself in social situations, you are perceived as being equally competent in business circumstances. (Don't ask me why!)

Follow up with everyone you meet. It's sad when both parties are expecting the other to call or email or text to arrange a follow-up meeting. Put it at the top of your To Do list. But do so with some thought; remember, you're connecting and building relationships. What I do is send the person some snippet of information, a card, or one of my many free resources—something beyond a mere email. I mention our meeting and highlight what I would have found particularly interesting or engaging about the encounter. You guessed it—as often as eight times out of ten, the other party responds and the foundation is laid.

Connecting requires you to be open to business 24/7. I've made connections in the checkout line in the supermarket, on flights to foreign destinations, at networking events, and via the Internet. My wife taught me one of her practices—which she refers to as "Wall-marketing." Since there is always a Wal-Mart nearby, we make it a point to make contacts every time we go there or to any other store for personal shopping.

When you are networking, you will find some people who are challenging to connect with and others who connect with you very well. Many of those outgoing personalities will also be involved with other activities you may have in common through volunteer programs and other common fraternal organizations.

You won't know who will become great lead-generators or best friends to you and your business until you go out there and find them. Get started networking; figure out how you can help them get rich, and the payoff will be that you will too.

Summary

Networking is a skill developed and perfected with use. The most important qualities involved are building trust and helping others with business referrals. Networking keeps you connected and motivated in your business cause. In the next chapter, we will get more deeply involved with community service by discuss-

ing how and when to give of your time by volunteering in activities that benefit the community you work with.

Chapter 14

VOLUNTEERING

*"The best way to find yourself is to lose yourself
in the service of others."*

— Gandhi

Let's recall the childhood story we likely all heard about Johnny Appleseed. It's a simplistic tale of a man who wandered America planting apple trees. Johnny was more than just simply volunteering to help. He was proactively helping the world for many years to come—even in ways he never realized. To this day, his legacy continues. When we think of how helpful an apple tree is, we can get lost in what a noble mission Johnny Appleseed had—how giving to others first was his goal. Most types of trees can become a home, even a sanctuary for insects, birds, squirrels, and even reptiles. They provide cover to plants and grass from the winds and rain. They can even be used for shade to help us truly enjoy a picnic with family and friends.

Maybe Johnny Appleseed could not envision how much those trees would do for thousands, even millions, of others he would never meet. He would never see those trees grow to maturity, and never partake of their fruit. He would never bear witness to their providing shelter for animals and food and support for others. He was simply a role model who volunteered most of his lifetime to giving to others.

Make no mistake about it—almost all of us love to volunteer as well. We feel good helping out our community and school programs. We strive to join long-standing fraternal groups, such as the Lions Clubs International, that were formed for the sole reason of giving. What we will find in this chapter is that nothing is more fulfilling than giving. It is one of the highest commitments we can have to stay motivated, maintain a balanced life, and strengthen our very being.

Community Needs

We've all heard the quote, "It takes a village to raise a child." I would argue that it also takes a village to nurture and empower a successful, satisfied, and happy adult. Therefore, as an adult yourself, and regardless of whether you seek material, emotional, or spiritual wealth, you must learn to foster and embrace your own support community to reach the highest of heights on your journey through life.

The word "community" may mean something different for each person reading this book, but no one can deny that we each need a support system to help us when we are overwhelmed, to uplift us when we are down, to lend a word of wisdom when we are attempting to choose our path, and to rejoice with us, even over the little things—if we want to experience true wealth in every area of life.

The reciprocal is also true; we must learn to meet the needs of others who can't achieve their life purposes unless we step up and become part of their vital communities. One of the greatest gifts that the recent economic crisis gave us was a new paradigm of community living and support. We are finally recognizing that we cannot do it alone. Community and collaboration are the order of the day.

You will either learn to live in and create a community, or you will find yourself falling behind. With that in mind, I present several tenets for creating community:

- Open-hearted boundaries clearly communicated

- Direct, honest, straightforward communication

- Taking personal responsibility for your own feelings

- Giving everyone the benefit of the doubt

- Not taking anything personally

Watch for these opportunities in your own life. Make a

mental note of where you are allowing your boundaries to be crossed, not communicating directly, or blaming others for your feelings, and where you are jumping to conclusions or taking things personally.

There is no action to take now other than awareness. All of these attributes will directly affect your ability to foster a core network of community and will have a direct negative impact on your overall wealth.

For now, simply become aware of these attributes and strive to improve them as you network, volunteer, and become part of a community.

Fraternal Organizations

People have always been drawn together by common interests. Fraternal benefit societies or organizations are an organized form of gathering people together who share common interests and ideals. Lodge associations, the Lions Club, and the Kiwanis are organizations that aim to meet the needs of communities on a local and global scale.

Giving is more than receiving. The concept of giving or philanthropy includes many types of giving. Giving helps you protect your mental and physical as well as financial health. When we give more and volunteer to do things, we are able to make new friends and contacts and really create a better network of business for wealth. No matter how small you may think your gift is, it can make a huge difference both to the organization and the people it serves. Moreover, social and relationship skills are increased during the giving process. When you give, you are regarded as a person of purpose—and that keeps you mentally stimulated, adding more zest to your life. In addition, when you consider your goals and interests, you live a more enjoyable, richer, and more fulfilled life while giving.

Everything in life supports the benefits of giving—science says people's sense of happiness is greater when they spend relatively more on others than on themselves. As the Dalai Lama notes, one's own happiness is dependent on the happiness of others. And as Mahatma Gandhi said, "The best way to find yourself is to lose yourself in the service of others." In other words, giving happiness to others means greater happiness for us.

Fraternal organizations were originally formed so people who shared a common bond could help one another—typically that bond was religious, ethnic, or occupational. Today, these organizations still help people socialize and come together as a community to celebrate their common bond. Fraternal organizations also offered insurance benefits to their members that cover loss of life, sickness, or accidental injuries.

Hundreds of such groups existed in America during the nineteenth century and flourished throughout the twentieth century; today, however, many of these organizations are disbanding or downsizing. The main reason is that while these groups were once united in specific philosophies, they did not always stress racial equality, religious freedom, or gender equality so when they failed to change with the times, younger generations lost interest in them. That said, many of these organizations have become more politically correct, they continue to focus on helping others, and they provide wonderful networking advantages. The bottom line for benefiting from a fraternal group is to attend one, give a little, and gain a lot in return.

Some fraternal and similar organizations you might consider joining include:

- Lions Club

- Rotary International

- Chambers of Commerce

- The Benevolent and Protective Order of the Elks

- Kiwanis International

- The Freemasons

- Knights of Columbus

- Civil Air Patrol

- Loyal Order of Moose

- A volunteer fire department

- A military auxiliary such as the Coast Guard

- Junior Chamber of Commerce—Jaycees

- LinkedIn and Meetup.com (the digital age version of fraternal groups)

- Twelve-Step programs like Alcoholics Anonymous

Each of these organizations varies, but by just joining one, you can take your networking to a much higher and more sophisticated level.

Summary

This chapter was about how you can remain motivated through volunteering. The next chapter will provides some ways you can keep challenging yourself to grow by speaking at events, writing an ebook, and attending mastermind groups.

Chapter 15

CHALLENGING YOURSELF

"Don't let the fear of striking out hold you back."

— Babe Ruth

We all must stay motivated. We must constantly seek self-improvement. We must remain involved with activities that challenge us. There is always room to grow and improve, so if we are dormant, we are regressing and losing steam. There are many things we can do to keep us busy, excited, and motivated. But we have to *do* them. If you challenge yourself with something you thought you could never do, you'll quickly find that you can do anything. You will discover that the very thought of a challenge is one of the strongest motivators you can have. As actress Cicely

Tyson has said, "Challenges make you discover things about yourself that you never really knew."

Whether you are a mentor or seeking to become a mentor, you must constantly be increasing your knowledge and awareness of the ever-changing world of real estate investing. In this chapter, I will challenge you to do four things that can help to increase your investing acumen through balancing in-depth research with opportunities to explain what you've learned. Those four things are writing an ebook, blogging, never passing up an opportunity to speak in public, and starting a mastermind group. These are probably the best continuous activities you can be involved with to maintain a high degree of motivation.

Writing an Ebook

The purpose of writing an ebook is to establish yourself as an authority on your topic—in this case, real estate investing. An ebook is an excellent prop to give away at one of your seminars. It can also be used as a *freebie* online where people can download it and, in return, you get leads to contact. If you are trying to make money writing an ebook, you will find, just as with publishing a larger hardcover book, writing is easy—marketing is tough. That alone gives greater rationale for leveraging it as a prop or lead generation tool. Your secondary motivation for writing the ebook is that you will elevate your research to a new level, and the result will be a book that provides value to others while highlighting to them that you are an expert in your field.

The guideline for writing an ebook is five to twenty pages in length if you are giving it away for free or thirty to seventy-five pages if it is for sale. It should be shorter than a regular book because ebooks are designed to capture and hold the reader's attention for quick learning about a specific topic.

The first thing you need to do when you embark on writing an ebook is to get your thinking right and believe in yourself. You must believe that you have at least one sincere message to send your reader. I've never met anyone who didn't have one rock solid idea he or she was dying to share with others, so go ahead and share it. The most popular topics for Real Estate Investing ebooks are:

- Beginner's guides

- How-to instructions

- Buying with no money down

- Cash flow

- Distressed properties

- Passive income

- Flipping homes

- Private money

- Building Wealth

Pick the topic you are most passionate about because that keeps your motivation level at its peak. Then try to align it to one of the most popular topics listed above. For example, the area I am most passionate about is mentoring others so the title I chose, *Making Others Rich First*, was based on two of the topics: How-to Instructions and Building Wealth.

If writing an ebook seems like a daunting process to accomplish, you can use a number of resources to ease your task. I recommend you consider using a publishing coach such as Patrick Snow (www.PatrickSnow.com) who specializes in helping authors write their ebooks and bring them into the marketplace.

So, the first method for staying motivated is to write about something you are passionate about. Another way to write about your fondest topics is to write short articles online in the form of a blog.

Blogging Your Way to an Audience

Writing is a key method for staying motivated because it requires you to express ideas, strategies, and solutions in a structured way that makes them easy to understand. In many cases, writing will require you to do additional research that you might not have done on your own. That research will help you, just as it helps your audience. You will find that writing blogs is much simpler and more acutely to the point than writing an ebook.

Blogs (online journals) are much more than a place to post your daily thoughts and ideas about real estate investing. Blogs give you a significantly greater Internet presence because search engines love them, and the keywords you use in them will help you to be found in searches. By the way, if you didn't know already, "blog" is just a truncated word for the original (not so interesting) term: web log.

The best way for real estate investors to use blogs is to post articles that contain the keywords and buzzwords we use most in our business in order to increase traffic. Here are some of the top targets:

- Sell house fast

- Sell home fast

- We buy homes

- We buy houses

- Cash buyers

- Need to sell home

- Sell house for cash

- Sell home for cash

- Sell without a realtor

- Sell vacant house

- Private money

- Hard money

- Distressed property

- No money down

Quite a few blog sites exist to choose from, but the most popular are Blogger.com and Wordpress.com. If you are a beginner and do not want to mess with code and html, go with Blogger, but if you want more control and do not mind messing around with some code, then Wordpress will offer you more options. Both of the above sites also have a lot of information on blogging, or you can simply type some keywords into Google for a plethora of results.

Consider reading books on the subject such as *ProBlogger: Secrets to Blogging Your Way to a Six-Figure Income* by Darren Rowse and Chris Garett. Also note that many published authors also have their own websites with a lot of great free information.

Some of the most popular places for you to look at examples of blogs or write your own, besides on your own website, are:

- www.reiclub.com/realestateblog/
- https://www.biggerpockets.com/renewsblog/
- www.deangraziosi.com/real-estate-forums/
- www.fortunebuilders.com/blog/
- https://realestateguysradio.com/blog/
- www.dohardmoney.com/blog/
- www.123flip.com/blog/
- https://justaskbenwhy.com/blog/
- blog.memphisinvest.com

- thinkrealty.com

- www.biggerpockets.com

I suggest you begin with the blog company you are going to use for your information. For example, if you plan to use Blogger.com, then do your research there first and review blogs that match the search "How to blog." That way you are learning on the site you are planning to use, so you will see examples of what can be done.

One of the biggest motivations for writing an ebook or blog is what you will get out of it: freedom of expression, organized and structured thoughts, and confidence in yourself. As you continue writing to stay motivated, you also begin to build greater confidence in your areas of expertise. You will grow the desire to express yourself through opportunities to speak at group meetings, networking events, and even seminars. Writing and speaking are mutually motivating because you are living and breathing real estate investing. Even if you have a fear of speaking in public, the progress you make through writing will prepare you to be bolder and exude enough confidence to say "Yes" to speaking opportunities.

Speaking Opportunities

Public speaking holds the key to many opportunities professionally and personally. In no other medium can you build your confidence and growing knowledge of real estate investing than by speaking to a group. Every talk you give is an opportunity to present information, products, services, and viewpoints to an audience. Speaking is also a great method for building your reputation and expanding your reach to other investors, contractors, lenders, and new investors who are seeking out a coach or a mentor to help them also get on the road to riches.

The best way to stay motivated is to write and speak about what you are most passionate about. Speaking may not come naturally at first, but your confidence will shine as you continue to take advantage of each new chance to speak to a group.

Every presentation should be focused on a key purpose. As a speaker, are you looking to present information, offer product information and samples, or shape viewpoints and persuade listeners to take a particular action? It is important to consider your purpose, but also your audience's purposes and needs. If you have little or no connection with the audience, it may not be worth the time, but also consider the old adage, "No exposure is bad exposure." It boils down to asking yourself, "What is my time worth to me, and what is the long-term value of this public speaking engagement?"

One of the best ways to get started is to go "back to basics." By that, I mean address the most common investing terms, deal structures, loan types, and returns on investment in deals you specialize in. One of my "back to basics" talks that I use over and over is my explanation of the three things it takes to make a deal: knowledge, time, and money. Each time I give it, it comes out a little different, a little bit better—and I feel the confidence growing in myself each time.

If you are giving an informational talk, make sure you provide accompanying written copy for the audience members. Brochures, presentation slides, speaker notes, and business cards can all assist you in ensuring that your talk transfers sustained information to the audience. The handouts you use will also increase exposure for you and your business activities. Do not think only on the large scale for public speaking/presentation opportunities; the same tools work well with boardroom presentations, one-on-one or small group sales presentations, and large, diverse venues and audiences. A well-laid-out presentation should be persuasive to the audience without being pushy or demanding. For example, I commonly use my discussion on "The Three Things It Takes to Make a Deal" when I'm talking to contractors or wholesalers in groups of one or two. The talk is about structuring a deal, but the inside information I want them to know is whom to call first when they find a deal or need a buyer or private money to help them move a property.

When you have an opportunity to speak at an event, you will find that the majority of participants are looking for something. Some are just looking for information, but others may be looking for guidance. Many want to have their needs met effectively, be that by investing in an apartment complex, buying tax liens, or finding a resource to access hard money, qualified renters, or maximizing their tax refunds. Knowing what the audience is looking for can help you tailor your talk and supporting documents to their needs. The most productive speaking engagements will be those where your goals and those of your audience find synergy. The best place to determine that is by discussing your audience with the event organizer.

Your speaking engagements can also easily be converted into promotional material for marketing yourself. They allow you to post videos, photos, testimonials, and thank you notes. All these, and PowerPoint presentations, are easily converted for use on websites and in email marketing. They can also be readily converted to YouTube videos.

A speaking engagement can also provide the opportunity to get information from potential investors and existing clients to build a better Customer Relations Database for marketing campaigns. Never fail to take advantage of opportunities to further your marketing efforts.

When you initially begin your speaking engagements, you will probably be at a small discussion group, a networking event, or a Real Estate Investors Club meeting. And it's okay to start out small and grow. After that, however, the opportunity to speak is something that must be actively sought out, not passively awaited.

Work on the presentations with smaller groups and hone your speaking skills before looking for large venues. To get more exposure and opportunity, speak with trade show promoters, industry leaders, community organizations, and chambers of commerce; let them know of your interest in speaking about real estate investing, your credentials, and the areas in which you are considered an expert speaker. And besides your growing confidence in writing, from blogs to ebooks, you can also submit papers for conferences and proposals for presentations.

Every chance to speak about real estate investing is also an opportunity to learn, grow, and refine your presentations and industry knowledge. Seek honest feedback from those who attend, and use that feedback to improve. If a formal survey is possible, use one; if not, garner information through social interactions after the presentation. Investors love to talk about deals, so they are an easy crowd to talk to. Public speaking about real estate investing will allow you to increase your business reach and reputation, as well as your personal reputation and value when coupled with refining speaking skills overall.

Speaking and writing are essential for motivation and self-growth. However, a fourth area is probably the most beneficial way to grow as an investor. That is by holding or attending mastermind groups. These groups are the ultimate area for support, motivation, and increasing your knowledge of real estate investing.

Mastermind Groups

As an entrepreneur, you should find a way to be involved directly with a mastermind group in order to sustain your investment portfolios, validate that you are on track, and participate in discussions with other investors who are closely associated with the type of real estate investments you are making.

Socrates is well-known for his belief that all growth takes place through discourse—the process of discussion. Unfortunately, our American model for formal academia has determined that the limited hours of instruction will consist largely of one-directional lecturing. But high achievers, entrepreneurs, inventors, and many successful investors throughout history have shared insights in small groups that have fostered discourse and opened the doors to ever greater success. One such entrepreneur I would like to talk about is Henry Ford.

Henry Ford did not invent the automobile, nor did he invent mass production manufacturing, yet he was one of the greatest forward-thinking entrepreneurs of all time. Henry married a very special lady, Miss Clara Jane Bryant, in 1888. They lived on a farm for a few years before moving to Detroit where, after eight years of mechanical tinkering, Henry completed a self-propelled vehicle with a gasoline engine that he named the Quadricycle. It took another twelve years before Henry was able to open the Ford Motor Company and launch the Model T.

Henry never received support from his family and friends. None of them believed in his foolish dreams. It was actually Henry's wife, "Miss Clara," who supported him and believed in his vision for so many years. She is the one who suggested that he, and several of his friends, assemble a mastermind group to help him grow that dream into reality. It was in that mastermind setting, with like-minded individuals, that Henry found validation, expertise, and instruction on how to bring together the combustion engine automobile with mass-production manufacturing. Henry never forgot the love and support that made him who he was. And he made sure the world knew it in 1938.

His idea of the "motor carriage" was a complete success and continued to be manufactured and sold for almost twenty years. After another ten years of successful automobile production, Henry was invited to New York City, where he would find acclaim as "Man of the Year" for his successful revolution of the auto industry by mass production technology. When asked in an interview how great this day must be for him, Henry replied, "The greatest day of my life was when I married Mrs. Ford."

It is amazing how one person's world can be changed when just one person totally believes in him and supports him. It did more than change Henry Ford. It changed the world. Ford's mastermind group included such brilliant minds as environmentalist John Burroughs, businessman Harvey Firestone, and inventor Thomas Edison. Later, it also included aviator Charles Lindbergh and U.S. President Warren G. Harding.

Successfully run mastermind groups beget successful entrepreneurs and investors. The concept is as old as human culture. Ancient Greek teachers, such as Socrates, Plato, and Aristotle, surrounded themselves with others who would challenge their own thinking in order to expand their knowledge.

Around the same time Henry Ford achieved his success, in 1937, Napoleon Hill wrote his timeless classic *Think and Grow Rich*. In the book, Hill explained the concept of the master mind as a "coordination of knowledge and effort, in a spirit of harmony, between two or more people for the attainment of a definite purpose." He further added, "No two minds ever come together without, thereby, creating a third invisible, intangible force which may be likened to a third mind." This was the initial explanation for the *mastermind*.

Quite often, as individual investors, we are too close to our own challenges to see the best solutions. So imagine having a permanent group of like-minded investors who meet every week for the purpose of sharing, brainstorming, networking, challenging, motivating, and encouraging each other. It's a win-win!

On one hand, it's like a think-tank that combines networking, brainstorming, and camaraderie, while on the other hand, it is a board of advisors purposefully designed to assist you in making the right decisions that need to be made. When you start or join a mastermind group, you will create deep and lasting connections with some incredible people. A Mastermind Group for real estate investors will challenge you to grow your portfolio to its fullest potential. In the crazy dynamic world of investing, it is easy to get sidetracked and waylaid. A Mastermind Group will you keep on track.

Sharing your ideas and alternatives within your Mastermind Group is a great way to brainstorm with people who are vested in your success. If you are not sure what to do next, what direction to go in, the collective power of the Mastermind is designed to kick in and get you back on track. Brainstorming will be met with receiving feedback from successful investors (who else would you surround yourself with?) on how to solve issues. You will be astounded at what you can accomplish through this type of support group.

Collaboration is the name of the game. Fellow mastermind members will help you to see the potential you are missing out on. And you will get great satisfaction from helping other investors in their acquisitions and creative financing.

Who should be in your mastermind group to make it successful? What characteristics should the members have? Members should be cooperative, dependable, loyal, and willing to share. Sensitive and perceptive thinking are an important part of being a group member. You must be sensitive to other people's wants and needs and to changes in their wants and needs.

I have been to a lot of successful networking events, and they were successful because they all had the simple objective to get to know other people. I hardly ever attend meetings just to drink coffee, tell a couple of jokes, take a lot of selfies, and collect business cards. I tend to be selective about networking events that will directly promote my investment activities. My most productive time is geared toward business activities and support for the members of my mastermind group.

A common format for a mastermind group is to select one person to focus on for the session each week. This is called the "hot seat," and it alternates every week. It is important for every member to be at every meeting. It's so much more than networking. *It's a commitment to a cause.* When I am in the hot seat, I send background information to all the members, via email, early in the week so they have a chance to review my situation and better understand my expected outcomes. Like a good coach, I call and email them every few days to remind them to keep this on the top of their To Do list this week.

Here are a few additional advantages to belonging to a mastermind group:

- **Advertisement:** Not only will the lonely feeling of running a business by yourself disappear in an instant, but you will have business advisors who will help and promote you along the way.

- **Collaboration:** In these sorts of groups, you can find people similar to you, who are perfect for working on a project together, or you will be a good match to someone who is in desperate need of help.

- **Networking:** By joining these kinds of groups, you will meet powerful people who have important contacts that can ease your work.

- **Learning:** The people you interact with share your interests. Every person in your group has a unique talent or skill that can help to resolve a problem quickly. Also, you get different perspectives, feedback, and input on your work.

- **Cross-Promotion:** When working with a team, not only do you help each other and improve your knowledge and skills, but through networking, you are promoted by your peers and vice versa.

- **Thinking Outside the Box:** Being in a group automatically motivates you to work a bit harder and think bigger. Surrounded by intelligent people, you will learn a lot of new things, gain experience, and push yourself to the limit to succeed in your own business.

- **Motivation:** Your peers will motivate you to work hard and give your best. There is nothing like being motivated to succeed!

- **Creating Valuable Friendships:** You will meet so many wonderful people who will help you and provide you with everything you need.

Finally, before you join a Mastermind group, decide on what type of group you want to belong to. Do the group members operate within the same areas of investing or is each person doing different deals? Do members have similar personality types or is there a conscious effort to have a mix of working styles? Typically, the more diverse the investors of the mastermind group are, the more value each member gets out of the experience. As someone once said, "If two or more of us do the same things, then one of us is not needed."

The investors mastermind group should be professional in nature, but personal growth is a welcomed side effect. This comes from the close relationships that are cultivated among members. If you are at a place in your investment practices where you are ready to mentor and be mentored, the decision to join a mastermind group is a no-brainer.

Summary

These last three chapters, Section IV, provided a healthy list of methods and activities you can get involved in to keep yourself highly motivated as well as recognized by your peers and your community. The final three chapters of this book, Section V, are about getting a return on your investment. If you are a mentor, you have so much to gain by working deals with new investors. As a new investor, you have the opportunity to learn from a mentor how to construct, manage, and close deals.

GETTING A RETURN ON YOUR INVESTMENT

*"Some people dream of success while others
wake up and work hard for it!"*

— Author Unknown

In this final section, we are going to address things you can do to achieve your dreams while also investing in others and how giving back lies on the same path you travel to get rich.

If you've invested a lot of time as a mentor in helping others get rich, you will ultimately pose the question to yourself: "What's In It For Me (WIIFM)?" A lot of answers come to mind quickly: "I made a difference," "I did something that matters," "I gave back," or "I really feel good about myself because I've helped someone else."

But there is much more to mentoring than these obvious "feel good" responses. If you structure a deal where you provide the money or the terms for a new investor, you can make some of your best deals ever.

All along, we have pointed out two straightforward principles: 1) you need knowledge, time, and money to do a deal, and 2) you have to find the deals. The return for mentoring is that you have mentees who will bring you deals. I've yet to find a newbie investor who had the knowledge, time, and money to structure a deal. Using myself to fill in the missing parts, I've found dozens of deals that make good money. The trade off is a win-win for both parties.

Helping others achieve their dreams allows us, as mentors, to gravitate to other areas of deals that we never would have explored. And it's not a selfish maneuver. It is simply being in the right place at the right time and being able to provide the missing piece to others who need your help.

In these last chapters, I will explain a little more about how wonderful it feels to help others achieve their dreams, always by taking the high road, and how mentors get rich in the process of helping new investors get on the road to riches themselves.

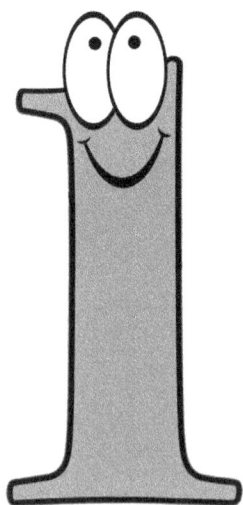

Chapter 16

ACHIEVING DREAMS

"All of our dreams can come true if we
have the courage to pursue them."

— Walt Disney

Achieving dreams is done by *magic*. Let me explain: Anything you can accomplish at a high level requires determination and hard work. Ask any magician—that's what magic is! There will be doubts and obstacles. And there will be mistakes. But where you apply hard work, there are no limits to what you can accomplish. Charles Kettering suggests that we should, "Believe and act as if it were impossible to fail."

Let's examine the potential you have to be a successful investor and then how to use that potential to accomplish your dreams. Almost everyone is seeking to become financially independent, and it is right that they should. You will be faced with many challenges when you get started; the challenge to learn, the challenge to dedicate time, and the challenge to buy your very first property. Each one of those challenges is an opportunity to discover the incredible potential you have to succeed. You learn by taking action on your challenges. Overcoming challenges is, in itself, the process of learning and continuing down the road to success.

Unleashing the Potential Within

As new investors, we start out shyly learning as we go, networking to see what others are doing to buy or sell properties, and cautiously signing up for training, boot camps, and property tours. We attend a variety of investor club meetings, Cash Flow games, seminars, and networking events. It's a challenging transition to enter into the arena where only experienced investors would normally gather. New investors seem to be learning much every day, and what keeps them going is that they know, deep inside, that they have the potential to succeed in this new realm of Real Estate Investing.

What is *your* potential? The simple answer is that you—in fact, every one of us—has unlimited potential—if you will just take action. Do not paralyze yourself by doubting your ability to succeed. A potential is not something you have to reach for—because it is already inside of you. You just have to unleash it.

I believe that the best way to tap into your potential is to use a mentor. I know you will be able to find a mentor who wants to help you find success. And if you find one who fits your strategy, you will both be winners because you will, as a team, find ways to take action and accumulate more and more real estate deals. Many times, a mentor will be happy to partner on a deal with you.

Your mentor can sense your potential and excitement. But she can also tell whether you don't have the passion needed to make it in the dynamic risk-heavy world of real estate investing. Your mentor can tell whether you are afraid and can help you overcome your fears. She will also hold you accountable for your actions and inactions. That is one specific area you need support on—especially when you first get started. If you can keep yourself motivated by the actions you take, your potential will appear before you as the fog of doubt dissipates right in front of your eyes.

A lot of newer investors never really get started because many of them find out that they really don't have as much passion as they thought they had. They never get going in the right direction because they somewhat stubbornly refuse to use a mentor. Some may have a false sense of pride, thinking they are strong enough and smart enough to figure things out for themselves. Don't let that happen to you. Seek out a mentor and she will find ways to keep you motivated. The bottom line is that doing lots of prosperous deals requires a lot of direction and effort. A mentor can provide the direction, but she cannot make you provide the effort.

In the very beginning, it almost always comes down to one simple factor: How *much* effort are you willing to give toward accomplishing your goal, fulfilling your dream, and reaching your full potential? As Sir Winston Churchill put it, "Continuous effort—not strength or intelligence—is the key to unlocking our potential."

So, how does one start making an effort? We make efforts by developing a business strategy, working with a mentor, evaluating options, buying a property, qualifying a renter, giving talks, writing blogs, teaching others, etc. Succinctly, we make effort by taking action.

I read several books that helped me get started. One of them you probably have read yourself: *Rich Dad Poor Dad.* It really got my blood boiling, and I could feel an excitement I never felt before. Then I followed up with a couple of books by Brian Tracy and Tom Hopkins—and oh, I could hardly contain myself. I was, in fact, on edge. If I hadn't started doing *something,* I think I would have burst. Yes, it really is that kind of excitement. Those books motivated me to seek out a mentor and find other investors I could learn from. So I did what any excited newbie would do—I googled "real estate investing clubs" to see whether I could hook up with others.

At www.reiclub.com, only one real estate investing club was listed in Hawaii, so that's where I went. I attended a couple of meetings and signed up for property tours in Dayton and Indianapolis. The first gutted, distressed home we stopped at I bought! I was excited; I had just taken action! Then when I got back on the tour bus, I called my wife—forgetting that at 10 a.m. in Indiana, it was only 4 a.m. in Hawaii.

"Guess what? I bought a property!" I told her, excitedly.

She replied, half-asleep, "Okay. How many properties have you looked at?"

I replied with firm enthusiasm, "One!"

My driven ambition was that I had to go through the entire process of buying a property, finding out the challenges of working with contractors, getting an inspection, understanding out-of-state property taxes, finding renters, and using a property management company. I had to take action! I needed to exploit the energy and potential I knew I had.

Deep inside, most of us think we are entrepreneurs. But on the outside, you have to show it, do it, and do it again until you get things done. You need to know why you're living—in order to really live! It is purely lack of effort that keeps "nontrepreneurs" from taking action. To realize and unleash our full potential is to fulfill the purpose of our creation.

After "learning the ropes" and getting a renter inside of my first rehabbed two story home, I began visiting Indianapolis every two months for the next two and half years. Your potential doesn't stop and your energy does not just subside after you make your first acquisition. Actually, that is when the real excitement begins.

If you want to be a multi-millionaire, you must be someone who takes action. The busier you are, the more successful you will feel. Nothing great happens by accident—it happens by work. You can become a successful investor and you can make your dreams come true once you realize that you do have this potential. And the way to use that potential is to take action and start doing your own deals.

You cannot deny the potential that lies within you. You may choose to ignore it, but it is still there—always there. Although most people won't admit it, almost all of them are convinced that they will fail; consequently, they never even get started. Once you open that fiery can of potential, you'll never get it closed again. You will find unbound abilities once you are off and running. As Og Mandino said, "I will strain my potential until it cries for mercy." Here are the four basic steps that will allow you to unleash your potential as a real estate investor:

1. **Believe in Yourself:** Most people do not realize that every person has the potential inside to be or do whatever he or she wants. You must understand this and believe in yourself. And when you truly believe in yourself, others will believe in you too. Example: Trust in yourself enough to make a commitment to go on a property tour. Set money aside to pay for the trip and commit to writing in a journal all the things you learned.

2. **Take Action:** Fear is a huge obstacle that can cripple the strongest physical specimen from taking the action necessary to get closer to his or her goals. It's vital to reflect on the fears holding you back and understand why they've been such a major obstacle, but the best way to overcome

those fears is to *take action*. Don't wait—and don't put things off. As my wife says, "There are seven days in a week, but none of them is *someday*." Example: Take action to buy a property within the next thirty days that you will use for passive income.

3. **Know Your Destination:** Know precisely what you want, the person you want to be, and have a target date set for achieving it. Again, consistent *action* is key to making progress toward your destination. Example: Commit to writing a blog about your new real estate investing career. Start by making a presentation at every other investors club you attend for six months. Then you should be ready to write those blogs.

4. **Use a Mentor:** A fuel is inside each of us just waiting to be ignited by one person who believes in us. Find someone who has experienced success whom you can talk to about your goals and discuss with him or her how to set up and design your road map. Having a mentor review your map is essential and just might be the spark that sets you on fire.

Unleashing your potential is what gives way to fulfilling your dreams and accomplishing your goals. You find out the power within you by taking action and putting yourself to work. Your goals are intermixed with your dreams and dreams don't work—unless you do.

Achieving Financial Independence

When you initially set your goals and strategy on what types of homes to buy and you decide on a price point to buy and an expected cash flow, you have no idea where that will really go because you have no direct experience with the complications of purchasing and owning real estate rentals. But once you get a renter in your first property—the light bulb goes on and you *get* it! That's when you say, "I can do this! This is what makes me happy! I know I can be a success!" And if you're like me, you start having bigger dreams like being so financially independent that you can truly and successfully quit your day job.

After your first few deals, it is expected that you will change your goals, change your business strategy, and reform your dreams. That is the magic of learning! More likely than not, your goals will move from amorphous fuzzy logic to taking on a fully recognizable shape. You begin to see how the numbers really work. Things will be so much clearer now, and you can more acutely define your real business plan—even if it's entirely different from your previous one.

The primary goal of your business, or any business, is to increase profit margins. For most real estate investors, that involves a never-ending effort to increase their volume of acquisitions and margins of profit. Since every deal requires money, it is necessary for you to find alliances and partners and lenders who will support or enable you to have money to turn more deals. Then a question that will ultimately surface is: "How many properties do I need?"

I initially discussed that back in the beginning of Chapter 1 when I explained the three things I needed to do to quit my day job. Remember? No debt, adequate monthly income amount from rentals, and a full year's salary in the bank. I needed enough properties rented out to ensure I had a specific amount of cash flow, which at the time was about $12,000 a month. But meeting your monthly quota and quitting your job are just steps in the process. You will set new goals, equally exciting and equally as challenging, as you continue to grow and share what you've learned with others.

Financial independence is a state—therefore, it should be your goal. You will attain that state when your properties are making enough income to pay your living expenses. It is not necessarily a state you can remain in for the rest of your life without ever having to work full time. Why? Because if you remain stagnant and cease to buy more properties, you might become less than financially independent due to inflation alone.

Even after you become financially independent, that may not mean you're actually "rich." It just means you don't have to work for someone else. There is still a lot of room to invest in more properties to reach a higher state of wealth. That is what I hope you are reaching for. Seek to be wealthy. Uncle Sam wants you to be wealthy. He gives you tons of tax breaks to be wealthy, and the last thing he wants is for you to be poor.

You will move from financial *dependence* (you need a job to pay for your lifestyle) to financial *stability* (you can pay all your bills on time) to financial *independence* (your passive income pays for your lifestyle) to financial *freedom* (where you can just buy anything you want to support your more extravagant lifestyle). I'm just saying: Financial independence is really not quite enough. Even after I was able to quit my job because of the passive income I had, I still had to do a lot more to enrich my lifestyle and move to a wealthier state of financial freedom.

What are *your* portfolio goals? Whatever that number is—whatever that amount of monthly passive income you wish to be at—once you achieve financial independence, you have only achieved your primary goal. You've proven your potential to reach your star. But there are other stars beyond that you want to reach. It's not the amount of money you need for your independence—it's the amount of money you need to enjoy your freedom.

Someone once said that achieving success is not the key to happiness, but finding happiness is the key to success. I have learned through many successful deals that if you love what you are doing and are passionate about it, you have, in fact, found your sweet spot—your happiness.

Keeping Contacts for Life

Whether you're already twenty years into investing or just starting up, retaining the loyalty of your peers and contacts is crucial, and keeping your reputation for being easy to deal with needs to remain as clean as you can make it. You will find that making good real estate investment deals is part art and part science. There are some specific things you need to do, and then there are creative ways you can make them happen. The best thing you can do is always to leave your client and your contacts smiling.

I've always tried to build win-win relationships so I can keep the door open to more deals with those I've successfully worked with before. I've always tried to make my renters happy because if I don't, my property is at their mercy. When you are an independent investor or a successful mentor, you are going to have a lot of people you'll want to keep happy. You should try to connect with them as if your future depends on it. Most likely, it does.

Here are some things you can do to help keep the doors open and your contacts happy:

- Provide leads and contacts to show how much you respect their success.

- Pay attention to names, pets, religious preferences, and birthdays.

- Use gifts as a reminder to how much their friendship means to you.

- Be quick to own up to your own mistakes and apologize for misunderstandings.

- Never talk bad about others. Take the high road and focus on the positive.

- Return calls and emails promptly and stay in touch.

- Invite them to a networking event.

- Always do what you say you are going to do.

- Take them out to dinner and spend quality time listening to their business.

- Keep current with them on Facebook.

- Always find a way to ask, "What do you think?"

- Say something positive about their websites.

Your personal and communications skills reflect your character. Do these things consistently to make your contacts always think of you as trustworthy, supportive, and an excellent friend. Always show your peers and contacts respect and appreciation. It is the most important thing you can give them. Always make yourself the better friend. The only difference between being average and being excellent is you!

It's All in the Follow-Up

As a real estate investor, you are going to get leads and new contacts—lots of them. How quickly you respond is even more important than how smartly you respond. Just being in front of a client is more important than having all the right answers. Returning a call right away is more important than waiting until you know all the answers. Following up with leads and prospects is the most undervalued thing that investors fail to do. Let me give you an example.

Have you ever bought something from a salesperson whom you didn't even like? Of course you have. We all have. My wife has a favorite jeweler who not only has unique creations but he repairs and modifies jewelry to his clients' satisfaction. He's an artist and he knows how to make his clients feel happy. Well, a few days before our anniversary, I had a short window in which to buy my wife a new piece of jewelry. I went to the store only to discover that the jeweler was out for lunch. I had to work with a different saleslady who didn't even know my wife, and from how she answered my questions, I felt uncomfortable dealing with her. She just didn't have that "care" factor, so I really did not want to deal with her.

But here I was with an anniversary coming up, so I had to make a purchase. As we looked through countless earrings, I became frustrated with where she was leading me. Eventually, I found something I knew would be just right. The only reason I bought from a salesperson I didn't even like was because she was *there*. I didn't want to talk to her or help her get her commission, but I had to deal with her and her attitude just because she was the only one present. Just being present, it turns out, is even more important than being good.

The same thing applies to following up with contacts, prospects, and leads. When you respond right away, and get in front of your lead, you have the upper hand on others who might even be much more qualified than you are. Following up fast is more important than taking your time to put all the information together.

In the real estate investing business, you are going to find that there is very little competition to being the first to follow up. Investors love to talk to other investors, share their knowledge, and offer deals. Try to make it a practice always to be the first person to call. I didn't say email, tweet, or text. I said call. Being second in this business is no different than being in last place.

Your first goal when you gain a lead—such as an investor who is trying to quick sell properties or an out-of-state investor interested in your area of expertise—is to get in contact with the person right away. Do this within twenty-four hours maximum. It's really best if you do so within thirty minutes. Otherwise, people get distracted, life hits them, they start thinking, someone talks them out of whatever it is you're offering, another offer comes along, etc.

If you don't get a home number right away, find the person's email address; that is always a fair place to start. Email is non-threatening and allows you to provide the person with some good content. If you do send email, then follow up with a phone call. My experience is simply to call on the phone ASAP and then follow up immediately with a text. After that, send an email with more detail. The first person in front of a client is usually the person who will be working a deal.

Start sending emails to your leads that offer free information or solutions to their problems. That information will vary depending on your target market. For example, let's say you're targeting people with an ad campaign like "We buy houses!" Your lead's problem is going to be that he doesn't have enough leads, his offers are too low, or he is having trouble following up with leads himself. Send him information explaining that you have the solution to his problems.

Remember, you don't have to be the best—you just have to be the first. On first contact, you should be humble and polite, ask direct questions, and explain why you are qualified to help. Being pushy or brash doesn't get you anywhere—except hung up on.

The best advice I can give you for following up is simply to be friendly and pleasant to talk to, to be able to explain the numbers in common language instead of complicated formulas, and to be able to articulate your knowledge of the types of deals at hand that your lead might be most interested in.

Having a great follow-up formula will get you more deals than you can imagine, and the only way you get great at it is practice, practice, practice. You should be on the phone as much as possible—speaking and texting. Both are active methods of follow up while email is simply passive, uninteresting, and will eventually end up at the bottom of someone's email inbox. The real estate investing business is dynamic—it is anything but boring. You need to be dynamic, know how to build creative deals, and make offers to buyers and sellers every single day. I will end this chapter with the best quote I remember from one of the greatest salesmen of all times, Tom Hopkins, who says you must, "Follow up, follow-up, follow up—until they buy—or die!"

Summary

This chapter was about momentum building with a discussion on unleashing your potential, how to have clients for life, and understanding the importance of following up with others you wish to make deals with. The next chapter discusses real estate ethics and the importance of always delivering on what you promise.

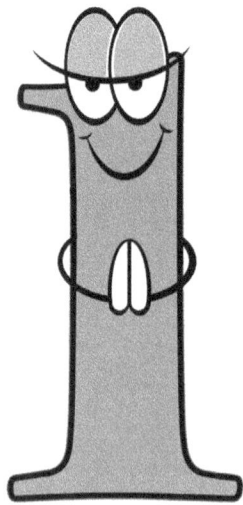

Chapter 17

TAKING THE HIGH ROAD

"The high road is always respected.
Honesty and integrity are always rewarded."
— Scott Hamilton

When we put on the mantle of responsibility for helping others with real estate investing, we must also don the armor of moral and legal consciousness. The last thing we intend is to get people into bad situations, mislead their good intentions, and violate their trust. The simplest way to be ethical, productive, and positive is to have a mental attitude focused solely on winning—and winning by playing by the rules.

Whether you are playing for yourself or helping others, you are playing to win! You should not think in terms of money—but in terms of winning. Again, return to your goals and objectives: your goal is to be rich, and your objective is to win with each deal you work on. And what's the best way to develop a winning attitude and a winning brand? Helping others get rich or achieve their goals makes you a winner! It's an important part of your brand because people want to work with winners.

Winners are poignantly focused, morally sound, and walk on an ethical foundation. A lot of people distinguish between morals and ethics, saying that morals relate to how we treat people we know, while ethics are about how we treat people we don't know. Ethics are how we build a society—by taking the high road. Do not let your character be stained in any way. If you keep yourself clean all your career and then suddenly do one tiny unethical act, you are stained forever. It is a stain that cannot be removed or even dyed out of the visible garment of your character.

We remain ethical to ensure that we are viewed the way we want to be viewed and in a way that is pleasing to us. This entire chapter is about being ethically sound, investing in others' success, and over-delivering on what we promise.

Presenting the Present

Wherever you are at in your goal to become financially independent, you have the opportunity to give and receive presents.

You can give *yourself* as a present to help others, or you can give yourself a present by using a *mentor*. You may even want to do both since even when you are mentoring others, you can always use mentoring yourself. Either way, you personify your desire to enhance and accomplish dreams. When we help others, we are giving them a wonderful present, but even then, they are giving us a present in return since we will feel good about helping them and also likely learn more about our business. Both givers and receivers then become winners. To integrate further this two-sided concept of presents, I'm going to go back to my basic qualifier that you need time, knowledge, and money to make a deal in real estate.

So, yes, you need all three, but exactly how much of each one is needed? If you only have one of those three, you can eventually make deals. The deal requires all three, but if you are a beginner, it only takes one. Let me share with you a story about a sophisticated investor who had no money or knowledge when I first met her and how she became a successful real estate dealmaker.

When I presented an opportunity to Alicia, whom I had met at an investors' seminar in Indianapolis, the present came with an investment opportunity. She had no *money* to invest, but she had something most people do not. She had the burning desire, the energy, and the focus to change her mindset and invest her *time*. As a matter of fact, Alicia had a lot of time, and she quickly became a master of managing herself because she had first learned how to manage her time.

341

I was living in Hawaii at the time, but I had just begun a series of trips visiting the Indianapolis metropolitan area every two months over the course of three solid years. When I first met Alicia, she told me she was living in her car and had undergone a very unfortunate series of incidents that limited her ability to find a good job and support her and her daughter properly. After we first met, we undertook a series of activities together that would change us both and make each of us realize our own and the other's greater potential.

We discussed basically the same things you have already read in this book about deal making. Then we toured the Indianapolis area looking at houses that might be investment opportunities. We analyzed the numbers and established the groundwork for which deals would fit my portfolio; this process gave her insight into how to build the vision for her own investment opportunities as she grew in *knowledge*. It was our *time* that enabled both of us to gain more knowledge about making deals. Each visit I made back to the area, I would meet with Alicia, and I was always amazed by how quickly she was growing in knowledge and how dedicated she was about investing her time.

Alicia began a two-pronged approach for building her character and self-confidence. She started working out in gyms every day, and ultimately, she got into such great shape that she was offered local modeling jobs. It was exciting to see her grow this way, but neither working out nor modeling—both time investments—were making her any real money. She still had to take small jobs wherever she could—just to make ends meet and have enough gas money to get around.

Through her growth in education and her continued attendance at seminars, networking events, and real estate investors' meetings, Alicia was presented with the opportunity to work with a capital investment group that also sensed her remarkable intensity, positivity, and dedication. She accepted a position and moved to southern California's coast to work with investors from all over America. Her success as a dealmaker and contributor to her local community made her a true hero to me.

Alicia changed my perceptions and practices about investing—forever. By working with her, I found that investing in others' success is the greatest *investment* you can make. I also found that helping others to succeed can be the greatest *success* you will ever know. And I never lost appreciation of the fact that we had both helped each other grow. Alicia is one of my genuine heroes. She has won on many levels, and she continues to succeed and also to give back by donating her time to important social causes. Her drive is feverish and intoxicating. She has made dreams come true for herself and others. And she continues to pursue bigger dreams—dreams that are bigger than she is—dreams that make her want to help others grow rich also.

To get rich and stay that way, you have to think better than an average person. That's the world we live in. Being able to affect and motivate others in some way with your skills, money, investment, and ideas goes a long way in determining how much better you can become and how limitless your journey can be. Help to present money and the other assets of time and knowledge to others, and in the process, you will secure a brighter future for them and yourself.

Investing in Others

I've always loved Mother Teresa's quote about helping others, "Some people come into your life as blessings. Others come into your life as lessons." Let's face it—there really is no person on this planet from whom we cannot learn something. When you invest your time and knowledge in others, with the purpose of helping them, you will really experience lessons in growing yourself.

When you are helping others to get rich, you are doing something great—not because of your power over others, but because of your ability to empower others to do better for themselves.

When I previously worked as a training director, I visited many military locations in the Pacific region where missions varied greatly, but positively charged motivators and trainers were always needed. This need arose from two primary factors: the constant turnover of personnel, and the continuing advancement in technology-assistance. One task I had was to transform an initial training program into recurring programs with established training objectives. After analyzing feedback from trainees by using *Kirkpatrick's Four Levels of Learning*, I realized that our training plans were not designed well enough to ensure that their outcome would enhance mission performance to the degree required of our target audience—the soldiers, sailors, airmen, Marines, and civil service personnel responsible for supporting their unit's mission and their host country's agreements that they were there to sustain.

One simple rewrite changed everything. As a group, we realized that it was not the training we provided that was essential, but the learning we should have been providing. Instructors and teachers everywhere can agree that it is in the transfer of knowledge and skills that we become successful as trainers. As a group, we worked over many months and rewrote our *training* objectives into *learning* objectives in all of our training plans and programs. Learning objectives were those measurable criteria that were mission essential for our trainees to learn and that we would test each trainee on by using a variety of verbal, written, or practice exams. If the student exhibited a 90 percent or better gain in learning, we realized that the training had been successful because the desired level of mission-oriented learning had been gained.

Instead of conclusively investing our time evaluating our own training, we learned that investing our time in evaluating what was learned by others was the smarter thing to do. It made them better soldiers, and it continued to make us more elite trainers.

You may be a third-degree black belt at networking, organizing activities, and speaking to a group, but the more time you spend actually helping new real estate investors, the bigger your world will become and the greater knowledge you will gain. Money really can bring happiness when you help to bring money into others' lives. If you have already learned how to reach your goals, then it's time to reach down and pull others up with you. You can start by making a commitment to invest in others. That commitment has to begin with an action, so here are some things you can do to invest your time in others:

- Decide to invest thirty minutes a day in others' growth and development.

- Develop or update a plan you have for mentoring others.

- Seek out a new relationship once a week and discuss mentoring.

- Pay attention and recognize when others can use help learning.

- Make it a point to introduce yourself to new investors at networking events.

- Take time to introduce new investors to other like-minded persons.

- Help others to articulate better and more clearly understand their "why."

- Show genuine interest in answering people's questions.

- Carve out enough time in your meeting to let the other person speak.

If you want to invest in real estate, you can change your life. If you want to invest in others, you can change the world. It makes that much of a difference. You're not really a genius until you have discovered how to help others unlock the geniuses inside them.

Do not forget that in either role, mentor or mentee, you have responsibilities to the other party. Here are some things you can do to support your mentor:

- Always show respect and appreciation for the time spent on you.

- Write things down as you hear them—you can ask more questions later.

- Ask a lot of questions—show true concern for comprehending new concepts.

- Honor your commitments and honor your mentor's time.

- Explain to your mentor how she can help you—she may not know.

- Do your best to accommodate your mentor's schedule whenever possible.

- Be yourself and describe things you do not know—don't bluff it.

- Take advice but be responsible for your own actions and development.

- Give back by referring others to your mentor or by being a mentor yourself.

You have an opportunity to make a difference once you give yourself the chance to make an impact on other people's lives. Mentoring is one thing that can set you apart from others and keep you rich in so many ways. Your decision to be purposeful about investing in people is what makes you different, and the best thing to do is to make such a commitment intentional. There is a truthful saying: "A man of success achieves his goals, while a man of significance changes his world." Your ability, which goes beyond providing for your own needs, will forever be appreciated and remembered. Success and riches are worthless if you don't have people to share them with.

Promising and Delivering

I am sure you've heard this one: "Under-promise and over-deliver." While I agree that making commitments is key to building character, under-promising sounds somewhat shallow and dated. To *under*-promise is just as nonsensical as to *over*-promise. A promise is a promise. A promise raises expectations, and those expectations should be met. Providing responses that exceed expectations is the right way to prove yourself. The mundane but imperative point here is to live up to your commitments when you make a promise and to give a little more to prove what makes you different.

The world of real estate investing is opportunistic, but it is also fraught with hype, promises, old information, gamesmanship, poor performance, and telling partial truths. If you are in a deal with someone who breaks a promise, you should never deal with that person again. Some people are always on the lookout to take advantage of good people. Those spots don't change. You don't want to be like that because people will definitely pass it on that you are not to be trusted. That's the kind of stuff that makes deals hard to come by. Look for predictability in your deals, and only deal with those who deliver what they say they will.

In reality, the under-promise and over-deliver hype is pretty much sales gossip designed to motivate salespeople by falsely making them feel they make a difference in an area they really do not. The salesperson is the one who feels better, but the client—not so much. Here's why: Your clients will be ecstatic and fulfilled if you deliver and help them reach their goals as you promised. In behavioral studies, we've seen that over-delivering is pretty much always a wasted effort. That's because *meeting expectations* is what people are really looking for, and somewhat wary of getting, in the real estate industry. Almost everyone involved with these studies has repeatedly said that when someone went above what was promised, it had almost no value at all. Researchers have concluded that promises function in our minds as though they were contracts. Once we buy into a "contract," we develop strong expectations that it be delivered, but we do not desire more than what was expected. When people are delivered more than what was in the contract, they actually become more leery than appreciative.

Having said all that, make commitments and meet expectations and you'll be the winner, the hero, and the person others will want to work with again. And, honestly, how much better can it get than that?

In the real estate investing world, you need to ensure you have a positive working relationship with people. It is important to set expectations properly by consistently delivering what you promise. That is always a five-star endorsement.

Summary

Whether you are a buyer or a seller in a deal, it is essential to understand that even though you are investing in a deal, you are always investing in other people. You must always hold true to the contract you have with others in the deal, and you should do that with clarity and openness. In the final chapter, we'll look at how important it is to give back to the business. You'll discover how using a mentor will get you rich quicker and how mentors get rich in return. After all, the goal of a mentor in the real estate investing business is to make others rich, first.

Chapter 18

GETTING RICH—
THE RETURN

*"A wealthy person is simply someone who has learned
how to make money when they're not working."*

— Robert Kiyosaki

You may find great meaning in life as a real estate investor. After all, you have the opportunity to design deals that will benefit many others—not just yourself. You can help provide homes for those who would not be able to do it without you. You can foster job opportunities, show others how to increase their family wealth, and help the entire economy become more robust and efficient by making good deals and mentoring others to do the same.

As the seventeenth century poet and philosopher John Donne once stated, "No man is an island." In other words, when just one single person in the entire world feels better, *we* rejoice. We rejoice because it's *our* world—and that means a lot more than just you and me. It means *us*, children of a Higher Power, who were born with the imperative responsibility to care for one another. It is our job to protect one another, to share with one another, and to enable everyone with equal opportunities. It is the inherent calling of humanity to facilitate that responsibility actively and teach our children to do the same.

But it seems, sometimes, that not everyone got that memo. The media overshadows good deeds with stories of controversy, deception, terrorism, conspiracy, hatred, and evil. We don't see enough good behavior in the news for one very good reason. It's normal to have good behavior and help one another. It's not news! While life may not be fair, helping others should be.

Today, we are seeing an ever-growing exposure of benevolent acts in the news and on TV. Whether it has high ratings or not, it's endearing and touching to witness how very kind and giving some people are. It feels good because it brings us back to our roots—to the core of our being, where we know that giving to others is what we should all be doing. It makes us feel joyful deep in our souls. Someone once said that if you want to comprehend the meaning of being rich, then just count all the things you have in your life that you didn't have to buy.

Helping others to become wealthy enough to pursue their

dreams and make possible the dreams of future generations can be one of our fondest achievements. And it is with selfless effort that we should pursue it. It's not important that we ever get recognized for the successes we bring—because true achievement is anonymous.

This final chapter is about what we get in return when we help others get rich first. Please do not anticipate praise for your efforts. If you expect praise, you are going to be sorely disappointed. And don't expect referrals from your efforts either. Besides, you're really doing it for a couple of different reasons. You're learning more about processes and getting more opportunities along the way than if you were never involved at all.

You will experience situations you would have never known about or considered until you actually work on a project another investor is working on. You are going to learn more from helping others get rich than you would ever expect. And the education and profits you gain this way you cannot gain in any other way.

Learning is its own reward, but getting rich from it is an awesome benefit.

For Richer or for Poorer

When we mentor others, we do it with the intention of benefiting them and, in turn, benefiting the world. Everyone wins when a real estate investment mentor works with someone who listens and acts in a way that benefits his or her move toward wealth and financial independence. All of the parties involved will be richer and better off because of it. What is most important to know, as a mentor and as a mentee, is that we enter into this relationship for richer or for poorer—for better or for worse. In other words, we are entering a relationship with expectations, and sometimes, the partner fails to perform or deliver based on his or her initial promises. Sometimes, the chemistry is not there so we move on.

We know that even if we teach others, and they take notes and they can recite what we covered, we still cannot make them do the things they learned. We also know that when we teach others and they charge off in another direction than what we defined, they may fail because of unreal expectations. Our goal was to make them richer, but their choices may have made them poorer. The sad news, as I've learned from experience, is that, when this happens, they will blame anyone but themselves. I have had a few people actually blame me for steering them wrong when I was helping them, but the truth is that they did not do as they were advised. Underachievers will always blame others, and then they will try to spread bad news about you or other associates because of their pride and insecurity. Such situations just come with the territory. Don't let others' bad words and attitudes keep you from continuing to help others.

Whether you are the mentor or the mentee, please know that if you provide the money, the processes, the time, and the knowledge yourself, then you've actually failed. A mentee must achieve wealth through his or her own actions and accomplishments. If he or she does not, it will most likely be unattainable for that person in future endeavors or unmaintainable in its present state.

A mentor shouldn't provide the answers as much as he or she should provide the advice, direction, and review. Provide the motivation, the resources (human and otherwise), and let people do things themselves. It's very beneficial and paramount to teach people how to fish, thereby giving them a lifetime source of a means to an end, rather than giving them fish and just feeding or saving them for the time being.

Whatever each party learns out of the relationship is a benefit in one way or another. The financial status of the mentee is a direct result of the decisions he or she makes—not necessarily the result of the mentor. I state that because the mentor's role is not to make all the decisions but rather to guide and advise. The relationship was established between an experienced, trusted real estate investor giving advice and counsel to a less-experienced one. The goal is to offer guidance in the development of a business strategy and an action plan to progress in an area chosen by the mentee.

The end result may be great financial gains for one or both. Sometimes, however, there is financial loss because of poor decisions. For richer or for poorer, it is the decision of the less-experienced investor that will provide the end result. I keep reinforcing this point because there are ways to make it more likely that the relationship will end with great financial gain. Some ways to make sure you are on track to make both sides richer include:

- **Develop and agree on goals and objectives.** Make sure you can measure the objectives that you build. They are the walkway to successfully reaching your goal, and they must be scientific, in that, they do not lie.

- **Provide feedback for every element of advice you receive.** Advice or guidance is just that. But what could happen or what did happen as a result of accepting or denying the advice is what really counts.

- **Know each other's background.** Although I appreciate great motivational speakers and inspirational books, neither have hand-guided me to make the most important decision of reaching my investment objectives. My best mentors have actually been those who made lots of mistakes in their learning years.

- **Set both short-term expectations and long-term goals to reach.** You must be accomplishing things along the path if you are going to continue to be motivated throughout your endeavor.

- **Declare the style and frequency of meetings that works best for you both**. Being clear about meeting format, objectives, and expectations will establish greater commitment on both sides.

- **Don't shy away from your own expertise.** As a mentor myself, I know that everyone I work with has certain skills and knowledge I do not. Be willing to share your expertise so the experience can be full.

I'd like to compare the mentoring experience to a knock-down piece of furniture one buys from the store; let's say a sixty-inch high bookcase. The box purchased contains twelve pieces of wood, forty-two screws, twelve nails, two ounces of glue, and a set of instructions. The *goal* here is to enhance your home-based business by providing more space for books and an orderly capacity of storage for often-needed resources. The *objectives* are pretty much the set of instructions you find in the box. Some builders have no fear, so they jump right in and build without the instructions and everything looks okay. And even if there are four screws, eight nails, and one piece of wood left over, the builder discards them and is, for now, very happy. Other builders go one step at a time, ensuring that the foundation and framework are built as designed, and even though it may take longer, the end result meets their goals and expectations.

In this scenario, the *mentor* is the person who wrote the instructions and likely designed the bookcase initially. He already did his homework by working with experienced builders to gain knowledge on how to build a bookcase. He then designed a series of components and instructions that were reviewed, updated many times, and eventually certified by approval of the builders, who validated the building process according to the instructions. The mentees then are those people who assemble the bookcase. Some of them will follow the instructions completely, some will partially follow them, and others will not use them at all. It is the decision of the mentee/bookcase assembler that determines success or partial success.

Giving Back Is Growing Forward

Giving back is one habit that allows and fosters your growing forward. By following a philosophy of giving back and making a personal commitment to customer excellence, service to the community, and helping others, you increase your own growth rate. An important aspect of growing forward is being willing to take risks. Many of us shy away from doing that; however, it's important to note that there are reckless risks and there are calculated risks. Do you think the world outside of you will not go on without you? It's high time you started seeing the community as an automated system that runs on a self-generating electric engine. Since you are of great importance to the society, give back to it; shape your community to be what you want it to be for you, your friends, your family, and the generations to come. Find a way to channel your positive energy into the world around you and you will experience endless growth in your career, business, and life.

Because we live in an era of business when we must be aware of other people, we have a responsibility to lend a helping hand whenever possible—and, of course, when we do, it is always for the better. Not only are opportunities presented for your business to go extra miles when you learn the spirit of giving back—but wonders are worked for your business. By giving back, you create goodwill—everyone comes away with a sense of happiness and human decency—and that generates a wealth of motivation for you and your team to do more.

Giving back is also a smart business move that provides

great PR. Whether or not intended, giving back creates great publicity for your business—generosity leads to a positive image that simply cannot be replicated in other ways. It gets you noticed! Moreover, it makes people want to work to help you. When you give back to various people, you are able to draw in more talented and unique individuals who are eager to make their mark on the world and want to do that through you and your business. The result is a mutually-beneficial relationship that will lead to more good for you and everyone involved.

How You Get Rich in the Process

Have you ever asked yourself, "Why do the rich keep getting richer?" Most of the time, it is not because of something as simple as luck, their family's fortune, or winning the lottery. It is because they do things differently—including making others rich. They know how to leverage their investments in knowledge, time, and money to find themselves richer at the end of each deal. As we have shared throughout this book, you, too, can get rich by helping others when you do the following:

- **Partner in a deal with a new investor.** If it's money someone needs, use your funds as private or hard money so the person understands the methods and costs of using other people's money.

- **Take advantage of the many training scenarios you will encounter.** Understand that you are investing in yourself.

Do not see money spent on personal growth as an expense, but rather, as an investment in your extended capacity to do better deals in the future.

- **Absorb the risks involved.** Most investors do not get enough exposure to actual risk other than their own failure to conduct due diligence. Anything you experience outside of what you have known before is a major opportunity for you.

- **Make money the end result of business transactions.** Buyers and sellers understand one thing about a deal: how much money is involved. Don't hide anything about a deal. Every investor knows that each party in the deal is going to make money. Explain everything clearly upfront and no problems will arise when closing the deal.

- **Consistently review your goals.** Ask yourself whether you have helped someone achieve something within a certain time period.

The finest testimony to your success that you can have is to leave behind in others the desire and conviction to give the best of themselves to others.

Furthermore, never lose sight of the dream and business you intend building, and focus on getting the job done. Develop a network in the form of collective entrepreneurship that allows you and your associates to nurture and grow the business. Constantly train and support your associates. Train them on new products, technologies, and emerging trends, and support them with the state-of-the-art logistics and business practices that create the right mindset and morale for remaining focused and executing the business. There is no magic here—just simple rules that will lead to your and your team's success.

One of the most effective ways for you to help others get rich first is to validate or extend an idea they believe will achieve wealth faster. The return on your investment is that you can include others in your deals as well. Remember that knowledge, time, and money is the cornerstone concept for putting together a deal—but they don't all have to come from you. It doesn't have to be your knowledge or your time or even your money. All you have to do is be resourceful enough to leverage those three from any resource in order to put a deal together.

I have found that the road to riches is discovered on the path of giving. When you work with others to make them rich first, you should always determine the resources they have for making a deal. Then it becomes simple to figure out what they are missing and how you can provide that missing element. They will be so excited that someone took the time to enable them to make a deal. When you do that, with the air of giving and helping, you will change lives. And one of the lives you will change will be yours. When you work to make others rich first, you can become rich in the process.

A FINAL NOTE

Whether we are experienced or new to the world of real estate investing, we all play to win. And playing to win is important to our success and motivation. Helping others will invigorate your ability to win exponentially. You will find greater motivation when you play to share, play to grow, and play to help others first.

Smart players can achieve great wealth by investing in real estate. There are so many things we can do to win in this business. But please don't count all the things you do; just go out and do the things that count. Helping others should be the first thing you do because if you help others first, then everything else will fall into place.

I challenge you to jump at any opportunity to mentor new investors because while you are enabling them, you will be helping yourself grow. Knowledge is not power, but sharing knowledge makes everyone powerful.

I challenge you to look at your own path for investing and develop a recipe for how you can make others rich first. You don't have to be great to start, but you have to start in order to be great. I wish you great success in your real estate investments and in your investment in helping others.

ABOUT THE AUTHOR

Barry Wilmeth is a real estate agent in Pearl City, Hawaii. His passion is helping families buy their first homes because his strongest belief is that the initial key to building wealth is buying your own home. He is especially supportive of military families moving to Hawaii, and he volunteers his assistance at multiple military bases on Oahu. Barry is also a seasoned, active real estate investor. He is an author, a mentor, and a keynote speaker who helps homeowners and new investors develop strategies for continuing to build their wealth by investing in real estate.

Barry's initial investments in condominiums began in 2003 and then spread to buying and selling homes in 2011. Since perfecting his Lease-Option sales strategy, he has helped many new real estate investors get started by taking the time to explain the basics and mentor them through their initial acquisitions. Barry's no-nonsense explanations are easy to understand, and his sincere interest in others' success shows in every discussion.

Barry Wilmeth is a native of San Antonio, Texas, but he has lived in Hawaii since 1982. He is a Vietnam-era veteran with over twenty years of service in the United States Air Force, serving throughout the U.S., Europe, the Middle East, and the Far East. Barry has a Computer Science degree and a Masters degree in Public Administration (MPA) from the University of Oklahoma.

LET BARRY BE YOUR MENTOR

There is a big difference between coaching and mentoring. Coaches usually don't work for free. Coaches probably won't schedule their time around you. Coaches will more than likely work with you no matter where you are in becoming an investor.

Mentors work for results. Mentors generally don't work for money. Mentors will work with you on your schedule and help you review and rewrite your goals and objectives. Mentoring is a power-free, two-way experience where advice, knowledge, and teaching are conducted in an atmosphere of self-discovery.

Unfortunately, most people, for whatever reason, never actually ask for a mentor. Experience shows that many new investors go to a seminar, sign up for a boot camp, and then get an upsell for using their boot camp instructor as a coach. All of these experiences require an amazing amount of money and are designed using a progressive motivational set of experiences. Now there are some really great coaches, to be sure, but few are worth the high price they charge you. How will you know? What's your ROI (return on investment)? Look at how much you've spent and compare it to how much money you're making flipping homes or gaining in passive income.

Want to arrive at your destination without having to pay a heavy toll? Use a mentor who wants you to succeed. Mentors are winners who want to sponsor winners. It's not about the money—it's about *success*.

Barry has mentored many different investors and has never charged a penny. His approach is to help you review where you are, develop a vision of where you want to be, and then build a roadmap to get you there. He'll be there with you at every milestone as you move toward successfully investing.

Barry Wilmeth not only mentors new investors, but he also mentors investors who want to be mentors thcmselves. There is something special about giving back that makes a mentor feel like things are right in the universe.

Contact Barry at:

bmwgog@gmail.com

808.282.1090

www.MakingOthersRichFirst.com

www.BarryWilmeth.com

BOOK BARRY WILMETH TO SPEAK
AT YOUR NEXT EVENT

Barry has been providing real estate investing advice at seminars since 2012. He is a connector who knows how to interact directly with his audience. Barry's philosophy is to provide an *edutainment* (education plus entertainment) value while asking specific questions to ensure comprehension of the material he is presenting. His primary goal at functions is not speaking or training; it is simply ensuring the transfer of knowledge and skills—LEARNING.

Whether your audience is five people or a room of 250, Barry's personable delivery is designed to ensure you "get it." He injects personal experiences of failures and successes—both of which are key to growing. He provides views from new investors, sophisticated investors, and mentors who wish to give back.

When you are looking for a memorable, dynamic, and engaging speaker who leaves your audience wanting more, book Barry Wilmeth.

Contact Barry today and make your next event a success!

bmwgog@gmail.com
808.282.1090
www.MakingOthersRichFirst.com
www.BarryWilmeth.com

www.ingramcontent.com/pod-product-compliance
Lightning Source LLC
Chambersburg PA
CBHW060319200326
41519CB00011BA/1776